TypeTalk
VOLUME 1

by Ilene Strizver

A note from the Publisher:
In order to make this ebook as useful as possible to you, we have decided not to lock the file with DRM or other security measures. However, please keep this book for your own use and do not share it with others. If you know people who would benefit from this book, please refer them to *indesignsecrets.com/shop*. Thank you!

Get the PDF:
Thank you for buying this book! If you want a full-color PDF of this book, send us an email at *support@creativepro.com* asking for the PDF, along with your purchase receipt (or a screen capture image of it). By requesting the PDF, you accept that we may email you occasionally (you can unsubscribe at any time).

© 2020 CreativePro Network Inc. All Rights Reserved

ISBN: 978-1-950896-03-5

Designed by Ren Reed using Adobe® InDesign®

The typefaces used are Klinic Slab for the body text and Barlow Condensed for the chapter titles. Designed by Joe Prince, Klinic Slab is a contemporary, versatile slab-serif. Barlow Condensed is a slightly rounded, low-contrast, grotesk font superfamily designed by Jeremy Tribby.

Contents

How To Select the Right Type for Any Job	1
Anatomy of a Typeface	13
Italic vs. Oblique	15
Type Classifications	20
Eight Timeless Typefaces	35
Vertical Alignment	45
Horizontal Alignment	47
Fine-Tuning Your Type: Hyphenation	49
Hung Punctuation and Optical Margin Alignment	58
Creative Indents	66
Point Size and Letter Spacing	69
Kerning Principles	72
The Ins and Outs of Tracking	77
Why Distorting Type Is a Crime	83
Glyph Positioning and Baseline Shift	86
Know Your Hyphens and Dashes	92
The Definitive Guide to Quotes, Apostrophes, and Primes	98
Finessing the Details of Type: Trademark and Copyright Symbols	106

Choosing and Using Swash Characters	112
A Blizzard of White Space Characters	122
Typography for Presentations	124
Designing for the Aging Eye	127
Footnotes and Endnotes	133
How to Create Sharp Digital Type Images	135
Fun with Pattern Fonts	144

Introduction

I love type. In fact, ever since I was a little girl, type and typographic forms have fascinated me. Of course, I didn't really know what 'type' was then, but I always drew shapes resembling letters, and a bit later, hand-lettered posters for school. I remember carefully measuring the thickness of the strokes, as well as the distance between them—albeit with no real understanding as to what makes for even spacing and such. But even with little knowledge, my interest and passion in the letters of the alphabet was unwavering.

Going forward, I never knew that type, or *typography*, would become my livelihood as well as my passion. To this day, I can't go anywhere and not see type—font choices, spacing, and readability—all to the eye rolls of my friends and family. These days, it gives me infinite pleasure to have acquired enough knowledge and practical experience to be able to teach others about not only type, but how to use and integrate it in design, whether it be for print, the web, and any digital device or application.

I have been writing my TypeTalk column for CreativePro.com for over 15 years now. I've written about typographic fundamentals and usage, as well as specific typefaces and their designers, calligraphers, lettering artists, movie titling and motion graphics, eBooks, and type for children, seniors, and those with visual impairments.

It therefore gives me great pleasure to introduce this collection of articles I've written over the years for

CreativePro. As we all know, it's one thing to bookmark a blog post, and quite another thing to remember where it is later, just when you need it. This book will provide a handy typographic reference for anyone interested in type. So find a comfy chair, a nice cup of tea, and dig in and read this book either from beginning to end, or as an occasional reference for that unanswered question. Enjoy!

1

How To Select the Right Type for Any Job

One of the most important—and some would say the most challenging—aspect of graphic design is selecting the appropriate typeface(s). Whether it's for text, display, or something in-between, this process and your eventual choices contribute greatly to the final outcome and to whether it hits the mark and meets the objective…or not.

Every typeface has its own personality and conveys a different mood, message, or feeling. Display, or headline, typefaces are usually stronger and more assertive, sometimes trading legibility at smaller sizes for a more powerful impact. Typefaces intended for small text will usually emphasize legibility—the ability to distinguish one character from another—and therefore are subtler in design, with personalities that tend to whisper rather than shout. Then there are typefaces that can be used for both text and display sizes.

Knowing the intended size range is not enough to make a selection; there is a lot more to choosing (and combining) type designs than that! Here are some factors and unofficial rules to consider that will help you narrow your search and ultimately make appropriate choices.

Design Goals

The number-one consideration in selecting a typeface for any project is knowing your goals, or more specifically, the goals of your client. As a designer, your primary responsibility is to meet your client's objective using your design and problem-solving skills. It is not to make their job into your own personal award-winning design statement—unless you can accomplish both at the same time! Every design project calls for a different approach: an annual report might call for a typeface with a high degree of legibility that also captures the spirit of the company, while a travel brochure might need to evoke the allure of a foreign land; a book cover might need a type treatment that catches the eye and tells a story at first glance, while the inside text might call for a pleasing, legible text face that doesn't tire the eyes after long lengths of copy. In addition, a website or gaming app might call for type that quickly attracts and captures its audience and lets them know the mood of what is to follow.

HOW TO SELECT THE RIGHT TYPE FOR ANY JOB

This travel brochure (top) uses fonts as well as color to generate the vibe of Mexico. The annual report (bottom) has a similar color palette, yet is a much more serious yet still engaging treatment.

The cover of this book (left) uses type and image to express mystery and intrigue, yet the text inside is clean, simple, neutral, and legible.

The type used for this popular video game is designed to be easy to read at any size and resolution, from a smart phone to a large monitor.

HOW TO SELECT THE RIGHT TYPE FOR ANY JOB

Know Your Audience

In order to decide on the most appropriate typefaces for a job, it is essential to know the age, interests, attention span, and other demographics of your intended audience. Different typefaces (and type treatments) will attract a different audience, both overtly and subliminally. Children are drawn to easy-to-read, childlike fonts; seniors to larger settings that have more clarity and readability; teens to edgier, more expressive designs. Once you identify your audience members, think about how much reading you are asking them to do and what information you are expecting them to walk away with. Once you know the answer to these questions, it will be much easier to narrow down your typeface choices.

A children's book and a punk magazine, albeit both from the '70s, use very different typefaces and design treatments to attract and appeal to totally different audiences.

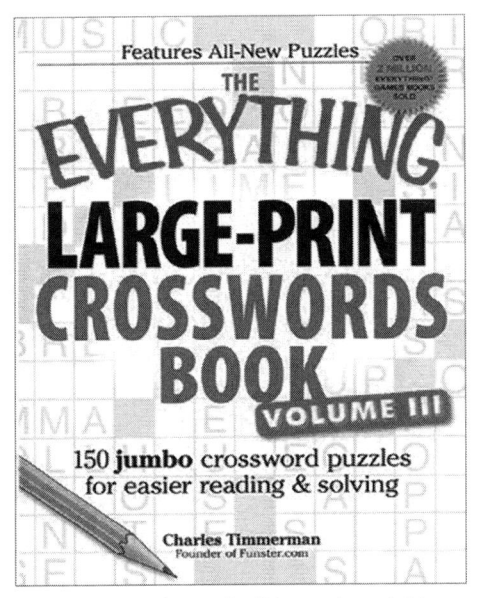

Keep the type large, legible, and readable when designing for the visually impaired.

What is Your Intended Type Size?

At the onset of any design project, it's important to know the intended type-size range of each chosen typestyle. Will it be used for a headline, subhead, running body copy, or all three? Will you be setting very small text for captions or credits? Or perhaps larger sizes for signage, trade show booths, or even a billboard? Or will it be applied to digital media with no fixed type size or even style? All of these usages require typefaces that are either intended for or usable at these sizes. Therefore, it's always wise to see for yourself how each one looks at both the smallest and the largest end of the intended size range.

HOW TO SELECT THE RIGHT TYPE FOR ANY JOB

While some fonts can be adapted to a broad range of sizes with the help of a bit of tracking or kerning, others will either become hard to read or lose the defining characteristics they were initially chosen for. So be sure to do your homework beforehand to avoid any surprises or unwanted results.

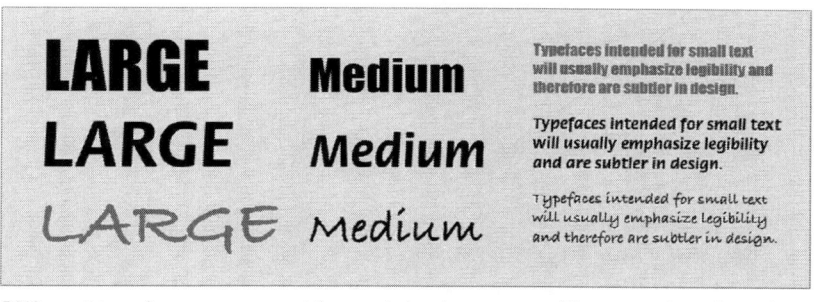

LARGE	Medium	Typefaces intended for small text will usually emphasize legibility and therefore are subtler in design.
LARGE	Medium	Typefaces intended for small text will usually emphasize legibility and are subtler in design.
LARGE	Medium	Typefaces intended for small text will usually emphasize legibility and therefore are subtler in design.

Different typefaces are meant for certain size ranges. Those settings in red are not being used within their optimal range. Set in Impact, ITC Flora, and ITC Bradley Hand.

Consider the Type and Background Colors

Think about the actual color of the type against its background when you're selecting a typeface, especially with text type. If you plan to use white or light-colored type on a dark color or image, the weaker design details (such as thin strokes) might not stand up to any potential ink spread, tint, or color screening or to a low-resolution environment, such as the web. In any scenario where the type size is small and the contrast between the type and the background is low (or even worse, unknown, as it can be with inconsistent color in digital media), choose a typeface or weight variant with heavier serifs and/or thin strokes, and a bit more overall strength and punch.

> The actual color of the type against its background should also be taken into consideration when selecting a typeface, especially with text type.
>
> The actual color of the type against its background should also be taken into consideration when selecting a typeface, especially with text type.

When placing type on a dark background, don't use a design with very thin strokes that might break up or start to disappear (left). Go heavy enough so it holds up and remains readable and inviting (right).

Is Legibility Important?

You'll often hear type described as being legible and/or readable. Although they both relate to the ease and clarity with which one reads type, they actually refer to two different things: *legibility* refers to the actual design of the typeface, while *readability* refers to how the type is set, or arranged. We'll concentrate on legibility, as it directly relates to selecting the right typeface for the job.

So are all typefaces designed to be legible? Not necessarily. You might say that legibility is important in direct relation/proportion to the length/amount of copy for which you need to hold the reader's attention. Display designs are generally used for a few words in larger settings where the objective is to be instantly noticeable and to convey a mood, feeling, or message, so legibility might not of primary consideration. But in any case, you need to know if this is one of the important to the goals of the project, and then choose accordingly.

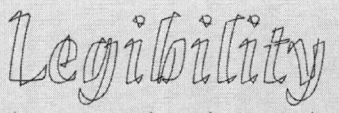

> **Legibility**
> Are all typefaces designed to be legible? Not necessarily. This is more important for text designs where the degree of legibility helps hold the reader's attention for the length of the copy.

The typeface on the left, Klee, is inspired by the expressionistic work of artist Paul Klee, and can be used in settings with small number of words where legibility is not of primary importance. In comparison, the typeface ITC Conduit, on the right, is extremely legible, and in fact can be used for both text and display settings.

Printing Method

When type is used for print, be conscious of the intended printing method and what effect it will have on the type, especially the thin strokes and counters. If reproduced with offset or digital printing with regular ink and no special effects, the results should be fairly true to the actual letterforms. But when using other printing methods, including letterpress, thermography, screen printing, embossing, or the use of metallic inks, the integrity of the letterforms might be affected, resulting in the thin strokes breaking up, counters filling in, or an other unexpected and unwanted outcome. In these cases, do your research before making your typeface selections, and allow for any properties that can affect the type's appearance when printed.

The surface upon which type is placed can have a major effect on how it appears: fabric can be a very coarse, porous surface for ink, while glass will absorb little or no ink, which just sits upon it and can bleed.

Print or Digital Usage

When selecting a typeface for print, make allowances for the kind of paper or surface it will be printing on. This is especially important when the desired typeface has extreme weight contrast with very thin strokes or serifs, or has small counters which run the risk of closing up. Different papers and surfaces receive ink differently, which can alter the appearance of the type, making it appear heavier or lighter, and in some cases, start to break it up entirely. For instance, newsprint and some textured papers are very porous and can make the type appear too light, while some coated papers and surfaces such as glass, plastic, and Mylar, don't absorb ink well, resulting in type that can appear heavier than intended. Take all of these factors into consideration when choosing a typeface in order to assure the best possible outcome.

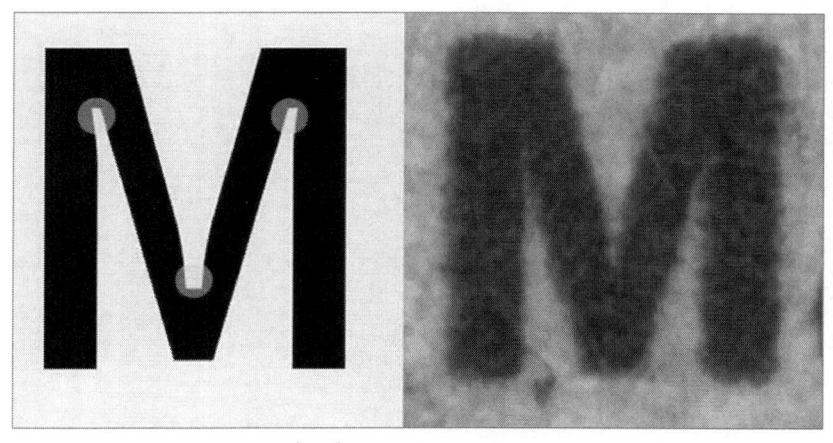

The digital outline of this M (left) has ink traps designed to absorb ink spread that can occur with newsprint. The image on its right is enlarged 6-pt phone book type, and is quite fuzzy and heavy.

Low-Resolution Environments

If the type is to be used in a low-resolution environment, such as some computer monitors, projected images, and porous newsprint, be sure to do some testing and/or research in order to know how it will perform before making your final selection. Once again, you might want to avoid typefaces with very thin strokes, small counters, sharp curves, and extreme angles, any of which might not reproduce well at lower resolutions.

High Resolution
Low Resolution

High Resolution
Low Resolution

This is an example of how different types look at both high and low resolution. Note the thin serifs of the upper setting (set in Consul) are breaking up, reducing legibility, while the sturdy low-contrast font used below it (set in Myriad) is readable at both.

2

Anatomy of a Typeface

As someone who at least sometimes (probably lots of the time) sets type, there's certain terminology you should know. I'm the first to admit that most explanations of the anatomy of a typeface (or parts of a character, as I like to call them) list many more terms than you need to know for everyday usage.

But here are the most commonly used (and most useful) terms when talking about type and the differences between one typeface design and another:

Baseline: The invisible line on which the flat part of characters sit.

Cap height: The height of capital letters from the baseline to the top of caps, most accurately measured on a character with a flat top and bottom (E, H, I, etc.).

x-height: The height of lowercase letters usually based on the lowercase x, not including ascenders and descenders.

Ascender: The part of a lowercase character (b, d, f, h, k, l, and t) that extends above the height of the lowercase x.

TYPETALK VOLUME 1

Descender: The part of a character (g, j, p, q, y, and sometimes J) that descends below the baseline.

Stroke: A straight or curved line.

Bowl: A curved stroke that creates an enclosed space within a character (which is then called a counter).

Counter: The partially or fully enclosed space within a character.

Terminal: The end of a stroke not terminated with a serif.

3

Italic vs. Oblique

Most designers and related creative professionals are familiar with the terms italic and oblique, yet there is still plenty of confusion regarding the differences between the two. While each refers to a slanted, or angled design, there are important distinctions between these terms, which in turn can influence their potential usage.

> ITC Legacy Serif Book   Univers Light
> *ITC Legacy Serif Book Italic*   Univers Light Oblique

Two typical examples of italic and oblique designs with their companion roman faces.

    Italics are an angled typeface that has different design characteristics from its up-right, roman counterpart. They are most often a separate yet complementary design, with unique features and, frequently, different character widths. Many italics have a somewhat calligraphic appearance, especially those that are designed for a serif typeface. Italics designed for a sans serif typestyle are often quite similar to their upright companion with the exception of a few (or more) differing characters, such as the lowercase a, g, and/or f.

> **Italic:** a different yet complementary design.
> *Italic: a different yet complementary design.*
>
> **Italic:** a different yet complementary design.
> *Italic: a different yet complementary design.*
>
> **Italic:** a different yet complementary design.
> *Italic: a different yet complementary design.*

Many italics are completely different designs from their companion roman typefaces, as illustrated by Adobe Garamond (upper); other italics are similar designs that contain a number of varying characters, such as the italics belonging to Enclave (middle) and Harmonia Sans (lower). Note the character width differences (as noted in the line lengths) between each pair.

Obliques, on the other hand, are simply slanted versions of their roman companions, with no major design differences other than their angle. They are most often found in sans serif typeface families, although not all sans serifs have obliques as opposed to italics, as noted above. (An important point to note is that although this is a broadly accepted naming convention, there are exceptions to this unofficial, yet commonly applied, rule. For instance, different versions of Helvetica can be found with the same slanted design named both italic and oblique.)

ITALIC VS. OBLIQUE

> **Oblique:** an angled version of the roman.
> *Oblique:* an angled version of the roman.
>
> **Oblique:** an angled version of the roman.
> *Oblique:* an angled version of the roman.
>
> **Oblique:** an angled version of the roman.
> **Oblique:** *an angled version of the roman.*

Obliques are a slanted, albeit optically corrected, version of their corresponding roman faces, and thus have similar line lengths.
Set in ITC Fenice, Glypha, and Avenir.

Professional-quality, "true-drawn" obliques and italics are not just computer-generated slanted versions of their roman companions, often referred to as "fake" italics or obliques, but are either hand-drawn or skilfully modified to optically correct the distortion that results from this action.

In his blog post entitled Fake vs. True Italics, font designer Mark Simonson describes the work that went into designing the italics for his Proxima Nova family, effectively illustrating the differences between the two. So remember: If professional typography is your goal, stay away from any fake or computer-generated obliques or italics (including those that are commonly created in word-processing programs), as they will degrade your typography and, thus, the overall design.

TYPETALK VOLUME 1

SOW SOW
SOW SOW

Computer-generated slanting (shown in red) results in distorted letterforms and inconsistent stroke thicknesses, akin to a funhouse mirror effect. True-drawn obliques (upper right), on the other hand, are proportionally balanced with correct stroke weights. Set in ITC Avant Garde Gothic.

So now that you know the difference between italics and obliques, how do you decide which to use? Both are commonly used for emphasis, as well as standalone usage. Most italics, especially the calligraphic variety, have a stronger contrast when used with their companion roman, compared to an oblique, which can be used in much the same way as italics, but has a softer "voice," if you will. Therefore, when doing your font exploration, consider how much contrast is required for the project at hand, and conduct your search accordingly.

ITALIC VS. OBLIQUE

When I had performed these wonders, they shouted for joy, and danced upon my breast, repeating, several times, as they did at first, *Hekinah degul.* They made me a sign, that I should throw down the two hogsheads, but first warning the people below to stand out of the way, crying aloud, *Borach nevola;* and, when they saw the vessels in the air, there was an universal shout of *Hekinah degul.*

When I had performed these wonders, they shouted for joy, and danced upon my breast, repeating, several times, as they did at first, *Hekinah degul.* They made me a sign, that I should throw down the two hogsheads, but first warning the people below to stand out of the way, crying aloud, *Borach nevola;* and, when they saw the vessels in the air, there was an universal shout of *Hekinah degul.*

The ITC Legacy Serif Italic used in the setting on the left creates a stronger, more noticeable emphasis than the Avenir Oblique used on the right. Excerpt from Gulliver's Travels, by Jonathan Swift.

4

Type Classifications

Type classification is a system used to divide typefaces into categories. This is useful for several reasons: to help identify them historically, to distinguish them visually, and to assist in combining them. Most typefaces fall into four broad categories: serif, sans serif, scripts, and decorative. But within these groups are many subcategories. The classifications system below will give you a basic understanding of where the many thousands of typefaces come from, and how they differ.

TYPE CLASSIFICATIONS

SERIF

Oldstyle

This category of typefaces originated between the late 15th and mid 18th century. It is characterized by curved glyphs with the axis inclined to the left, minimal contrast between thick-and-thin strokes, angled head serifs, and bracketed serifs (curves between the serif and the stem). Some typefaces in this category contain an e with a diagonal cross stroke.

SERIF > OLDSTYLE

ITC Berkeley Oldstyle
Adobe Garamond
ITC Legacy Serif

Belmo

Transitional

Typefaces in this category represent the 18th century at a time of transition between oldstyle and modern design. They have the following characteristics: the axis of the curved strokes is barely inclined or more vertical than diagonal, there is more contrast between thick and thin strokes than in oldstyle typefaces, and serifs are thinner, flat, and bracketed.

SERIF > TRANSITIONAL

ITC New Baskerville
Bulmer
Perpetua

Belmo

TYPE CLASSIFICATIONS

Modern (Neoclassical, Didone)

Originating in the late 18th century, this refined and more delicate style is characterized by high or dramatic contrast between the thick and thin strokes, curved strokes on a vertical axis, and horizontal serifs with little or no bracketing.

SERIF > MODERN

Bodoni Antiqua

Didot

ITC Fenice

Belmo

Square Serif

Typefaces belonging to this early 19th century style have very heavy square serifs, little or no bracketing, and hardly any stroke contrast. They are often geometric or square in style.

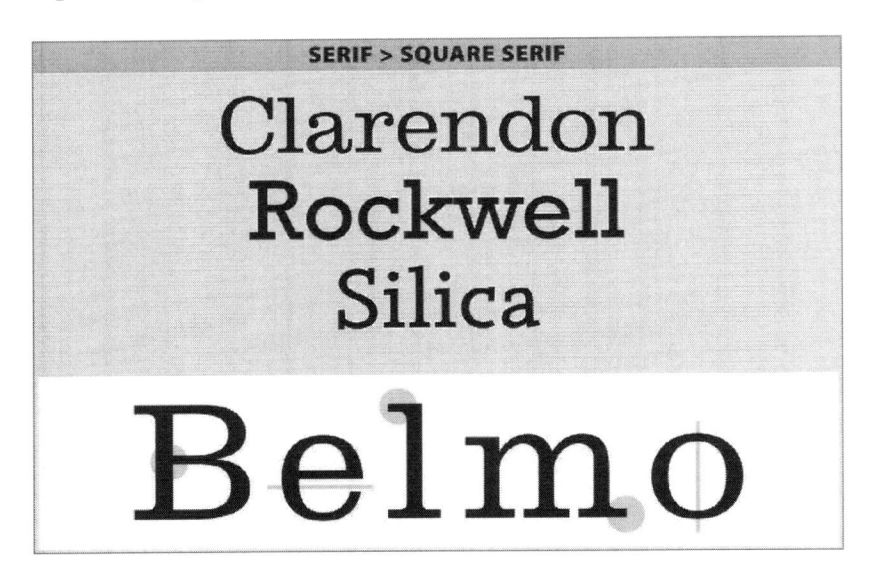

SERIF > SQUARE SERIF

Clarendon
Rockwell
Silica

Belmo

TYPE CLASSIFICATIONS

Glyphic

Glyphic type styles appear lapidary (carved or engraved) rather than pen-drawn in nature. They have a vertical axis, minimum stroke contrast, and often have triangular or flaring serifs.

SERIF > GLYPHIC

Friz Quadrata
Newtext
ITC Quorum
Belmo

SANS SERIF

Grotesque

This style was the first popular sans serif. Its distinguishing features are slight contrast in stroke weight, a squared look to some curves, a "spurred" capital G, and a double-bowl lowercase g. Later versions lost their squared curve, and have a single-bowl lowercase g.

SANS SERIF > GROTESQUE

Bureau Grotesque
Franklin Gothic
Helvetica

Bglmo

Geometric

These typefaces are based on simple geometric shapes, and usually including monowidth strokes and perfect circle rounded forms.

SANS SERIF > GEOMETRIC

Avenir
Bauhaus
Futura

Belmo

Humanistic

Humanistic type styles were an attempt to improve the legibility of sans serif designs by blending their structure with the classical Roman form. More simply, they are based on the proportions of Roman capitals and oldstyle lowercase, with an apparent stroke contrast, as well as a calligraphic influence.

SANS SERIF > HUMANISTIC

Frutiger
Gill Sans
ITC Stone Humanist

Belsa

TYPE CLASSIFICATIONS

SCRIPTS

Formal

These very elegant typestyles derived from the penmanship of the 17th century are characterized by flowing loops and flourishes with graceful, rhythmic strokes. They are most often connecting scripts.

SCRIPTS > FORMAL

Bickham Script
Edwardian Script
Snell Roundhand

Belmo

Casual

These scripts are designed to look informal, as though quickly drawn with a pen, brush, or similar writing instrument. Their strokes can be connected or not, and they tend to be warm, friendly, and relaxed.

SCRIPTS > CASUAL

Bianca
Bickley Script
Mahogany Script

Belmo

TYPE CLASSIFICATIONS

Calligraphic

This broad category of typestyles strives to imitate the writing or lettering of the calligrapher, whose work is hand-drawn for each job. Calligraphic typestyles often look as if they were drawn with flat-tipped pens or brushes, and they occasionally include the drips, spots, blotches, and irregularities inherent in the process. Their strokes can be connected or non-connected.

SCRIPTS > CALLIGRAPHIC

Ballerino

Ruach

ITC Wisteria

Belmo

Blackletter

Blackletter type styles evolved from the early handwritten forms of liturgical writings and illuminated manuscripts. This style went from writing to typesetting when it was used to set the Gutenberg Bible, the first book printed with movable type. Blackletter typefaces are characterized by a dense, black texture and highly decorated caps. The lowercase consists of narrow, angular forms with dramatic thick-to-thin strokes and serifs.

SCRIPTS > BLACKLETTER

Engravers Old English
Fette Fraktur
Goudy Text

Belmo

TYPE CLASSIFICATIONS

Handwriting

Handwriting typefaces are typographic interpretations of actual handwriting or hand printing. The stylistic range is extremely diverse and can be anything from a connected script or scrawl to quirky, bouncy, irregular hand printing.

SCRIPTS > HANDWRITING

itc Deelirious

Emmascript

ITC Kristen Normal

Belmo

DECORATIVE

This very broad category consists of typefaces that do not fit into any of the preceding categories. They're most often designed primarily for display and are meant to be distinctive, original, and eye-catching. They adhere to few or no rules, and they defy pigeonholing.

5

Eight Timeless Typefaces

Fonts come in and out of vogue, with popular typestyles constantly being replaced by newer, trendier designs. But even with the hundreds of new typefaces being released each year, there are some that don't seem to age, while continuing to serve their typographic purpose.

Here are eight typefaces that, in spite of having been around for dozens—and in some cases hundreds—of years, don't appear to have an expiration date any time soon.

ITC Machine Bold

This brawny, geometric, uppercase sans serif design was created in 1970 by the design team of Ronnie Bonder and Tom Carnase. It comes in two weights, but the Bold is a much stronger, more impactful design.

MACHINE BOLD

ITC Machine Bold is most effective when set with tight letter- and line spacing, as this tightly-packed appearance creates a dense wall of typographic texture that makes a powerful statement. ITC Machine Bold is excellent for posters, headlines, signage, and other display applications that call for a commanding, authoritative look.

Fette Fraktur

Fette Fraktur is a blackletter typestyle that was originally issued by the C. E. Weber foundry in Germany in 1875. As the translation suggests, Fette Fraktur has a fat, broken appearance. This forceful, historic design is noted for its dense black texture, extreme thick and thin strokes, and highly decorated caps, all evoking the look of the Middle Ages.

Although this style of typeface might seem to have a very limited application, Fette Fraktur has expanded way beyond what might have been perceived as it narrow scope. Its highly stylized, impactful appearance has become quite fashionable, and can be seen on book covers and magazine spreads as well as posters and movie titles. It also lends itself to very dramatic initial caps.

EIGHT TIMELESS TYPEFACES

Fette Fraktur is used sparingly, yet with purpose, making for a very stylish, eye-catching editorial spread. Courtesy of Nancy Campbell and Trevett McCandliss.

Linoscript

Linoscript is an elegant, readable, upright script that never seems to age. It was designed by Morris Fuller Benton in 1905 and released by American Type Founders as Typo Upright. It was renamed Linoscript in 1926 when it was integrated into the Linotype technology. Modeled on the then-popular style of upright French scripts, Linoscript has flourished capitals and connected lowercase letters with extravagant loops on the ascenders. It is ideal for a broad range of applications, including invitations, book covers, greeting cards, menus, editorial heads and subheads, and other uses requiring an elegant yet easy-to-read formal script.

TYPETALK VOLUME 1

The use of Linoscript for the branding of this television show definitely sets the tone: The elegant script representing the "housewives" contrasted with the image suggesting the apple that Eve ate (which got her exiled from Eden) combine to illustrate good vs. evil.

Clarendon

Clarendon is a slab serif (also knows as Egyptianne, a category of typestyle that first appeared at the beginning of industrialization in Great Britain in 1820). Originally designed by Robert Besley in 1838, it was reworked by Hermann Eidenbenz in 1953 for Monotype, and has been much imitated since.

EIGHT TIMELESS TYPEFACES

Clarendon

Clarendon is a timeless design that has never lost its contemporary feel.

With its chunky, geometric serifs and its assertive forms, Clarendon is a timeless design that has never lost its contemporary feel. In spite of its historic beginnings, Clarendon remains a typeface that is widely used in popular culture. It commonly appears in catalogues, on websites, book covers, and movie titles, as well as signage and posters. Clarendon is available in three weights: Light, Roman, and Bold. The lighter weights are legible in small sizes, and the heavier versions make a bold statement when used at larger sizes.

This attractive Kansas statehood stamp, designed in 2011, uses Clarendon.

TYPETALK VOLUME 1

ITC American Typewriter

Ever since the invention of the typewriter, font designers have created typefaces to emulate typewriter type. One of the most popular of these was ITC American Typewriter, designed by Joel Kaden and Tony Stan in 1974. Its release marked the 100th anniversary of the invention of the typewriter, at a time when the typewriter was the only device used for office communication.

> **ITC American Typewriter**
>
> Ever since the invention of the typewriter, typefaces have been created to emulate typewriter type.

    ITC American Typewriter retains the distinctive look of typewriter letterforms, but with improved legibility, especially for text. This typeface has a friendly, familiar appearance, with a touch of nostalgia. Since its release 40 years ago, ITC American Typewriter has never really gone out of style, and sometimes pops up in the most unexpected places. In addition to more traditional uses such as logos, branding, and packaging, it can also be found in fashion magazines, mobile devices, and even tattoos! Grungy typewriter fonts might come and go, but this classic is here to stay.

EIGHT TIMELESS TYPEFACES

ITC American Typewriter makes it to the big time: two covers of Vogue!

Century Schoolbook

Century Schoolbook is recognizable to many as the typeface we learned to read from. It originated from Century Roman, which was designed in 1894 by Linn Boyd Benton for American Type Founder (ATF). In 1924, his son Morris Fuller Benton designed a variation based on his father's design, and called it Century Schoolbook.

Century Schoolbook

Century Schoolbook is recognizable to many as the typeface we learned to read from.

TYPETALK VOLUME 1

Although it was originally designed to be an easy-to-read typeface for children's books, its extreme readability (open counters, generous character width and x-height, balanced weight contrast, and open letterspacing) made it popular for advertising as well. Its original design came in two weights (regular and bold); italics were added at a later date, making this a much more useful typeface. This sturdy design, with its appealing, inviting appearance, is still being used for textbooks, periodicals, and other applications requiring a highly legible text typeface.

> **WHO INVENTED THE WRITTEN WORD?**
>
> Well, as with most really, really important things, not everyone seems to agree. Especially the experts. But it definitely wasn't just a single person or culture, and we do know that the concept of a written language started more than 3,000 years ago—in more than one place on earth—and that it has evolved ever since. Mankind's tangible record of its daily existence dates back to the cave paintings of the Neolithic Age (Fred Flintstone times), but that's not really what we'd call a language, though in some ways we have come back to it full circle (see Pictogram, page 115). Actually, it is believed that numbers were created first, many thousands of years before letterforms, and were used to keep tallies of possessions like tools and livestock. Records that survive were created by making notches or slashes on materials such as wooden logs, animal bones, and rocks. These slashes eventually became the basis of Roman numerals, which exist to this day—you most commonly see them on grandfather clocks and fancy watches.

A page from GO: A Kidd's Guide to Graphic Design, by Chip Kidd. Century Schoolbook is used for much of the text.

EIGHT TIMELESS TYPEFACES

ITC New Baskerville

ITC New Baskerville is one of many contemporary type families based on the work of John Baskerville (1706–1775), a noted writing master and printer from Birmingham, England. This historic revival was designed in 1987 by John Quaranda and is an interpretation of the Baskerville style. ITC New Baskerville is an inviting, dignified, and highly legible classic that makes an excellent and very readable text face. The italics are particularly elegant and distinctive, with several unique and recognizable glyphs, including the lowercase v, w, and z.

ITC New Baskerville

ITC New Baskerville is one of many contemporary type families based on the work of John Baskerville.

ITC Franklin Gothic

Sans serif typefaces never go out of style. For that reason, there is a constant stream of revivals of older designs, as well as brand new originals to fill this ever-present need. But one family that will never be replaced is Franklin Gothic. Originally designed by Morris Fuller Benton in 1904 for the American Type Founders Company, this historic design still works well for both text and display, imparting a modern-day feel.

While there are several versions of this classic typeface, one of the most popular is ITC Franklin Gothic, designed in 1980 by Victor Caruso for International Typeface Corporation. This version retains the strength and vitality of the original ATF Franklin Gothic, with a slight increase in x-height for improved legibility. This series was followed in 1991 by a suite of 12 condensed and compressed designs drawn by David Berlow.

ITC Franklin Gothic works well for both text and a display. It is considered a standard for newspaper and advertising as well as in museums, film titling and subtitles, and logos. When set for text, it presents a clean, legible, and still contemporary appearance.

ITC Franklin Gothic

Originally designed by Morris Fuller Benton in 1904 for ATF, this historic design still works well for both text and display.

6

Vertical Alignment

Many people assume that numerically consistent leading results in visual balance (or they just don't give it much thought in the first place); thus, they often overlook vertical alignment.

For example, when you set a three- or four-line headline with an all-cap line, the space above that line appears to be (visually) smaller than the space above the lines set in upper- and lowercase (u&lc), even though they have the same leading. That's because capital letterforms take up more headroom than a line set in mostly lowercase, even with the occasional ascender. To make matters worse, the shorter the x-height of a typeface, the more extreme the inequity appears.

The solution is to adjust the line spacing of the offending all-cap line (and any others that appear uneven) so that it visually matches the rest. This might result in a line spacing value that is numerically quite different from the rest, but the goal is to make the line spacing of the text look the same optically, not mathematically.

> We offer a variety of
> web and interactive
> TRAINING CLASSES
> for every skill level.
>
> We offer a variety of
> web and interactive
> TRAINING CLASSES
> for every skill level.

I set the upper example in 32/35 (32-point type with 35-point leading), but due to the line set in all caps, the space above that line appears to be much less than between the rest. For the bottom example, I increased the leading of the all-cap line to 42—a whopping 7 points more than the rest. Set in Century Schoolbook Std.

Horizontal Alignment

Creating proper horizontal alignment is a bit more challenging than vertical alignment due to the subtleties involved, but it's just as important for producing professional-looking typography.

Software aligns characters by the edge of the character plus its side-bearing, which is the space added to the right and left of a character in a font to prevent it from crashing into other characters. The characteristics of the spacing of certain characters, such as a capital T, capital A, and the numeral 1, as well as periods, commas, apostrophes, dashes, quotations marks, and ellipses, will often create a visual hole or indentation at the beginning or end of a line, making that line appear to be slightly off-center. This occurrence is magnified in implementations of larger type, including centered headlines and subheads.

When this occurs, shift the line in question slightly to the right or left until it visually looks centered. The easiest and most precise method (and least problematic when changes are made to the size and font) is to kern the offending character to a space added before or after it until the line looks visually centered.

> An hysterical romp through the world of midlife dating—you just might find yourself laughing out loud!
>
> An hysterical romp through the world of midlife dating—you just might find yourself laughing out loud!

The top multi-line example is technically centered using Adobe Illustrator's Align Center command, but the second line visually appears off (too far to the left) due to the em dash at the end of the line, which has a lot of negative space above and below it. The horizontal alignment is improved in the example on the green background by adding two word spaces at the beginning of that line, and then using negative kerning between the spaces to fine-tune it. Set in TypeCulture Expo Serif Pro.

8

Fine-Tuning Your Type: Hyphenation

Hyphenated words are a necessary evil in most typesetting, especially in narrow columns in print. The downside is that they can reduce readability, particularly if there are many consecutive hyphens. But the upside is that hyphenation can create tighter, better-looking rags in non-justified margins, and can help achieve more even letter spacing in justified text by having more control over rags, making for a more pleasing appearance.

Designers and production artists might take for granted that their software will handle hyphenation (and other typographic) details in a professional manner. But while today's design software products are quite robust in their capacity to fine-tune type, it is up to the user to determine if, when, and how much to hyphenate, and to set the software preferences to behave accordingly. So how can you know how many hyphens to allow, and when? Read on, as the guidelines for controlling this important yet subtle differ for print and digital media.

In that quarter of the town, however, scarcely any shortcoming in dress would have created surprise. Owing to the proximity of the Hay Market, the number of establishments of bad character, the preponderance of the trading and working class population crowded in these streets and alleys in the heart of Petersburg, types so various were to be seen in the streets that no figure, however queer, would have caused surprise.	In that quarter of the town, however, scarcely any short-coming in dress would have created surprise. Owing to the proximity of the Hay Market, the number of estab-lishments of bad character, the preponderance of the trading and working class population crowded in these streets and alleys in the heart of Petersburg, types so vari-ous were to be seen in the streets that no figure, how-ever queer, would have caused surprise.

Narrow columns with no hyphenation can cause unsightly deep indents (left). A few well-placed hyphens can even out the rag (right).

Hyphenation in Print

Paying close attention to hyphenation in print is important, as hyphens are a fixed entity that can be controlled and tweaked, unlike on the web, where line endings can change for each viewer. Recognizing that hyphenation settings are sometimes based on personal preference and sometimes on professional style, it's generally considered acceptable to have two consecutive hyphenated lines in a row, but no more. This is because it reduces readability by making the eye-to-brain translation work harder. In addition, try not to have too many hyphenated line endings

FINE-TUNING YOUR TYPE: HYPHENATION

in a paragraph, even if they are not in successive rows, as this too will affect readability. Another suggested rule of thumb is that it is typographically undesirable to have two-letter hyphenation breaks at either the beginning or the end of a word, and thus a line.

NO HYPHENATION	DEFAULT HYPHENATION	CUSTOMIZED HYPHENATION
would have created surprise. Owing to the proximity of the Hay Market, the number of establishments of bad character, the preponderance of the trading and working class population crowded in these streets and alleys in the heart of St. Petersburg, types so various were to be seen in the streets that no figure, however	would have created surprise. Owing to the proximity of the Hay Market, the number of establish- ments of bad char- acter, the prepon- derance of the trad- ing and working class population crowded in these streets and alleys in the heart of St. Pe- tersburg, types so various were to be seen in the streets that no figure, how- ever queer, would	would have created surprise. Owing to the proximity of the Hay Market, the number of establishments of bad character, the preponderance of the trading and working class population crowded in these streets and alleys in the heart of St. Peters- burg, types so various were to be seen in the streets that no figure, however queer, would have caused surprise.

When hyphenation is necessary within narrow columns to improve a bad rag (left), using the default Hyphenation settings can result in too many consecutive hyphens, as well as undesirable two-letter breaks (center). Customizing the settings for a more conservative outcome will usually result in a better looking, more even rag (right).

Some people (designers and clients alike) dislike hyphenation and avoid it entirely. I caution against this all-or-nothing perspective, as the occasional hyphen in a mostly unhyphenated text can make a big improvement. For instance, wide columns can often go without hyphenations except for the occasional manually inserted hyphen to fix a bad rag here and there. In addition, setting text that contains numerous long words (such as medical or pharmaceutical copy), as well as text set in foreign languages with very long words (such as German), can result in a rag that is extremely deep and unattractive; in these instances, the addition of the occasional manually-inserted hyphen can improve the rag, making for a cleaner, neater appearance.

> It may be possible for a person to get progressive multifocal leukoencephalopathy (PML) (a rare, serious brain infection caused by a virus). People with weakened immune systems can get PML, which can result in death or severe disability. There is no known treatment, prevention, or cure for PML.
>
> ---
>
> It may be possible for a person to get progressive multifocal leukoencephalo-pathy (PML) (a rare, serious brain infection caused by a virus). People with weakened immune systems can get PML, which can result in death or severe disability. There is no known treatment, prevention, or cure for PML.

When setting copy with very long words, any width column can result in distracting, deep indent (upper). It only took one manual hyphen to improve this text block (lower).

FINE-TUNING YOUR TYPE: HYPHENATION

Setting Up Your Hyphenation Preferences

Today's design software allows you to customize the hyphenation settings to your liking. If you don't explore this option, you're stuck with the defaults, surrendering control of your type to your software.

The two main applications designers use to set type for print are Adobe InDesign and Illustrator, both of which have controls for hyphenation, located in the Hyphenation or the H&J panel. The default settings usually allow two-letter hyphenations (a no-no IMHO) as well as anywhere from three to unlimited consecutive hyphenations. This is an overly generous setting for most text, as it can result in reduced readability. At the bare minimum, I recommend changing the default settings to allow a minimum of three-letter hyphenations, and no more than two in a row. In addition, it is a good practice to deselect Hyphenate Capitalized Words, Last Words, and Across Columns, all of which can result in some unattractive and undesirable word breaks if left selected.

InDesign's Hyphenation Settings panel has several other options to help you control your type. If you don't want short words hyphenated, you can increase the Words With at Least option. Hyphenation Zone and Hyphenation Slider are two other settings you can play around with to adjust the location and quantity of hyphenations. I confess I do not alter these settings, preferring to manually adjust rags in order to have complete control. But for large projects with lots of text and multiple pages, you might want to explore them to

TYPETALK VOLUME 1

help automate your software to achieve the best results with the least amount of manual fine-tuning.

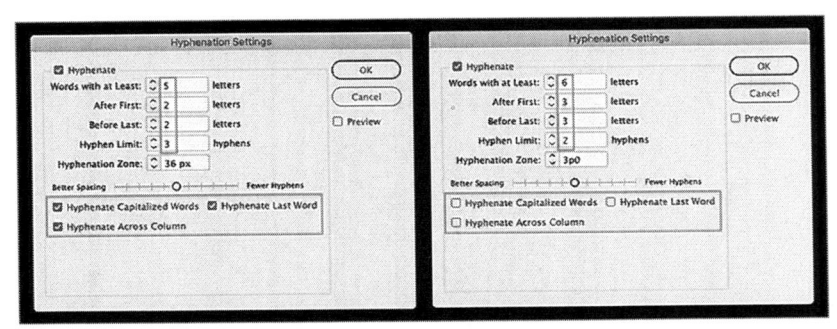

The default hyphenation settings in InDesign are shown on the left, with my suggested settings on the right.

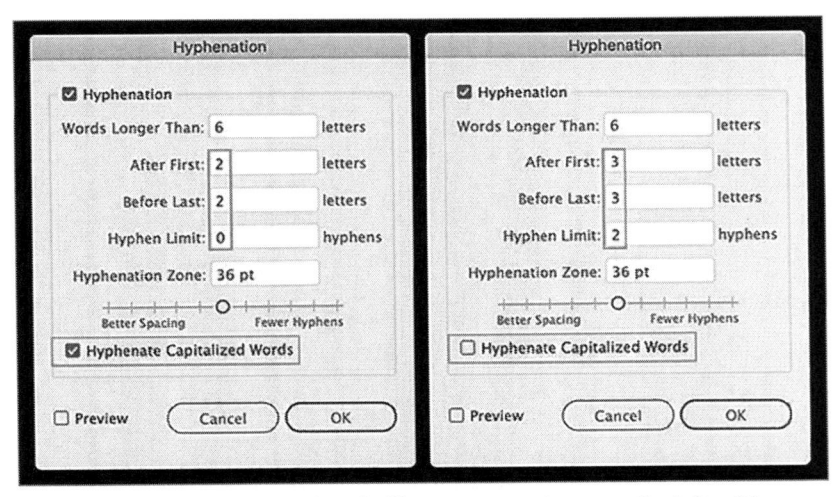

The default hyphenation settings in Illustrator are shown on the left, with my suggest settings on the right.

FINE-TUNING YOUR TYPE: HYPHENATION

When manually hyphenating a word within text, it is advisable to use a discretionary hyphen rather than a standard hyphen. A discretionary hyphen is visible when a word is hyphenated at the end of the line, but disappears if the text reflows and the word in which it's placed no longer needs to break, eliminating the need for the hyphenation. This way you will avoid those nasty "surprise hyphenations" appearing unexpectedly in the middle of a line. You can add a discretionary hyphen in InDesign by choosing Type > Insert Special Character > Hyphens and Dashes > Discretionary Hyphen or by pressing Command+Shift +hyphen / Ctrl+Shift+hyphen.

Discretionary hyphens, available in InDesign, can be found nested deep in the Type menu, towards the bottom of the column.

If tweaking your Hyphenation settings doesn't generate the results you want, try manually re-breaking the troublesome lines. If necessary (and if ethically possible), edit your copy (or have your editor do this) to achieve a better flow. If your layout allows, sometimes adjusting the width of the column ever so slightly will result in fewer breaks.

TYPETALK VOLUME 1

Hyphenation on the Web and Digital Media

Currently, most web browsers as well as the CSS and HTML standards applied to them do not support hyphenation. While it is true that some very current versions will support the automatic insertion of hyphens to break a line, most users (especially non-designers) do not have or use these versions, so it is safest to assume lines will break after a full word. The problem with this is in a narrow column, as well as with text set using very large words, there will be more line breaks than usual, reducing readability.

In order to minimize unsightly deep indents, I recommend adding a word space before and after both en and em dashes (but not hyphens) that appear in text. This way, the browser can insert line breaks at those spaces as needed to improve the rag, which would not happen without the added word spaces.

FINE-TUNING YOUR TYPE: HYPHENATION

They began to get real cream for me, do you hear that? And how they managed to get together the money for a decent outfit—eleven roubles, fifty copecks, I can't guess. Boots, cotton shirt-fronts—most magnificent, a uniform, they got up all in splendid style, for eleven roubles and a half. The first morning I came back from the office I found Katerina Ivanovna had cooked two courses for dinner—soup and salt meat with horse radish—which we had never dreamed of till then.	They began to get real cream for me, do you hear that? And how they managed to get together the money for a decent outfit — eleven roubles, fifty copecks, I can't guess. Boots, cotton shirt-fronts — most magnificent, a uniform, they got up all in splendid style, for eleven roubles and a half. The first morning I came back from the office I found Katerina Ivanovna had cooked two courses for dinner — soup and salt meat with horse radish — which we had never dreamed of till then.

When setting text for the web or other dynamic (changeable) media, it is a good idea to add word spaces around hyphens to provide the option of more word breaks. If this is not done, one can wind up with deep, unattractive, and very distracting line breaks (left). The added spaces will improve potential bad rags (right).

When type appears in any digital media (often referred to as dynamic, meaning the type and images can change size and appearance, as opposed to fixed, as in printed media), including web CSMs (content management systems such as WordPress), blogs, ebooks, apps, and kinetic type, do your research first to find out if hyphenation is an option, and if so, set the preferences to whatever the job and your personal preferences call for.

9

Hung Punctuation and Optical Margin Alignment

To hang or not to hang—punctuation, that is. The term hanging punctuation might not be familiar to some, as the related terminology in digital typesetting is optical margin alignment. They are actually a bit different, but both serve to accomplish the same thing: to create optically (as opposed to mechanically) aligned flush margins, whether they be both margins in justified text, or a single margin in flush left or flush right text.

Hung punctuation was used by Gutenberg in the Gutenberg Bible. All double hyphens (a variation of the single hyphen often used in blackletter typestyles) are hung into the right margin as shown in page from The New York Public Library's Gutenberg Bible, Book of Numbers, Rare Book Division.

HUNG PUNCTUATION AND OPTICAL MARGIN ALIGNMENT

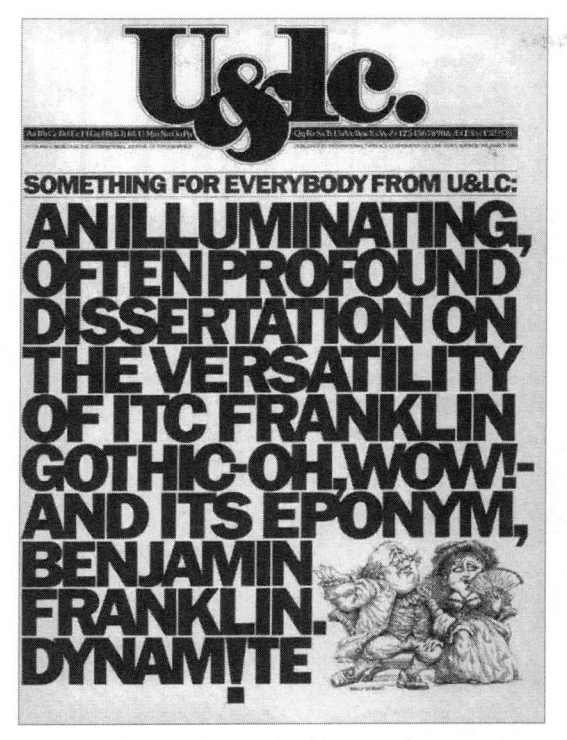

Herb Lubalin was known for his attention to every typographic detail, including hanging punctuation, as can be seen on the right margin of the text on this cover of U&lc magazine.

Hung (or hanging) punctuation refers to the practice of extending lines beginning or ending with certain punctuation, such as quotations marks, hyphens and dashes, periods, commas, asterisks, and any character that does not have a lot of vertical mass, into the margin of a flush edge of text to create the appearance of a more visually, or optically, aligned edge. The punctuation then appears to "hang" in the margin of the text. This is done because a line that begins or ends with these punctuation marks can result in a margin that looks uneven. "Hung punc" (as it was commonly referred to) was—and still is—considered an advanced technique that was done with regularity by experienced typographers prior to desktop publishing, but it became more challenging, if not impossible, to achieve in the early days of design software. This is no longer the case.

> → "We have so asserted our station, both in the old time and in the modern time also," said the nephew, gloomily, "that I believe our name to be more detested than any name in France."
>
> →"We have so asserted our station, both in the old time and in the modern time also," said the nephew, gloomily, "that I believe our name to be more detested than any name in France."

The optical alignment of this flush-left setting (top) is marred by the negative space created by the open quote that begins this text. The alignment is greatly improved by hanging the open quote into the margin (bottom). Excerpted from A Tale of Two Cities, by Charles Dickens.

HUNG PUNCTUATION AND OPTICAL MARGIN ALIGNMENT

> "We have so asserted our station, both in the old time and in the modern time also," said the nephew, gloomily, "that I believe our name to be more detested than any name in France."

> "We have so asserted our station, both in the old time and in the modern time also," said the nephew, gloomily, "that I believe our name to be more detested than any name in France."

The alignment of both margins in this justified setting is interrupted by the negative spaces created by the quotes, hyphen, and comma. When Optical Margin Alignment is applied, the punctuation marks hang into the margins, creating a neater, cleaner alignment.

Optical margin alignment is the term used by many of today's digital design programs, which uses hung punctuation to tweak the alignment of a flush edge (including letters, numerals, and symbols, such as a capital A, T, W, the numeral 1, and trademark symbols) to help pursue your aesthetic vision. That is to say, this sophisticated technique is not used to right a typographical wrong as such, rather, to assist in bringing out your personal taste and professionalism.

> → **Teachers open the door but you must walk through it yourself.**
>
> ← **Teachers open the door but you must walk through it yourself.**

InDesign's Optical Margin Alignment feature not only hangs punctuation, but any character, number, or symbol which needs adjusting to create a cleaner alignment. In this case, it is the capital T.

Optical Margin Alignment in InDesign

While it's not difficult to manually hang punctuation in headlines, subheads, and other large settings, many designers don't bother finessing text settings in this manner due to the impracticality of making dozens of manual adjustments. The good news is InDesign has the capability of creating a more optically aligned text margin with Optical Margin Alignment. This is a little-known but extremely powerful feature in the oddly named Story panel. When this is activated (it is turned off by default), not only is punctuation pulled into the margin for a more uniform appearance, but so are serifs and the edges of certain characters with overhanging strokes, as previously mentioned. InDesign gives you control over how much these characters extend into the margin for the entire text frame.

HUNG PUNCTUATION AND OPTICAL MARGIN ALIGNMENT

To set Optical Margin Alignment in Adobe InDesign:

1. Select the text frame, or place the cursor within the text
2. Choose Window > Type & Tables > Story (or choose Type > Story)
3. Choose Optical Margin Alignment
4. Adjust the point size as necessary to get the results you want

Note that the default setting for how far into the margin characters will extend is 12 point, but it can be adjusted, as it doesn't necessarily have to correspond to the point size of your text. Select a point size for the amount of overhang by starting with the size of the type and going up (or down) from there. Go by what looks good to your eye, not by the number; sometimes the ideal amount may be considerably larger than the size of the text.

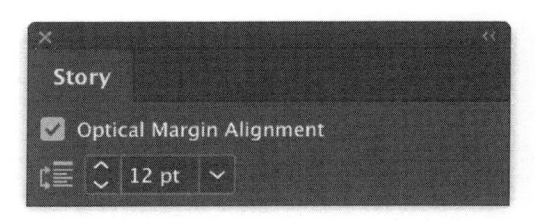

Optical Margin Alignment in InDesign is accessed via the Story panel (Type > Story or from its tab on the right in the Typography workspace). You can adjust the amount of overhang here as well.

TYPETALK VOLUME 1

Optical Margin Alignment in Illustrator

This feature exists in Illustrator as well, but it is greatly simplified; it can only be turned on or off with no ability to customize the value. Even so, if you are setting type in Illustrator, this does improve spotty, unbalanced alignment.

To set Optical Margin Alignment in Adobe Illustrator:

1. Select the text setting, or place the cursor within the text
2. Choose Type > Optical Margin Alignment

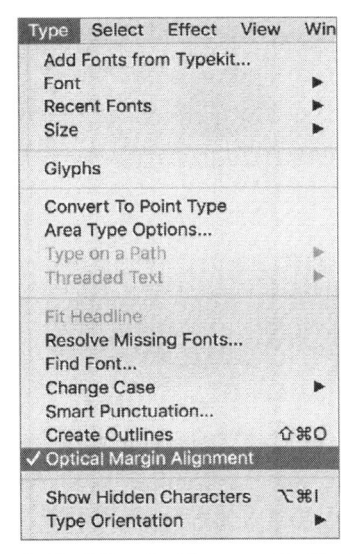

Optical Margin Alignment in Illustrator is accessed from the Type menu. It is either on or off, with no ability to change the overhang.

HUNG PUNCTUATION AND OPTICAL MARGIN ALIGNMENT

Helpful Hints

Here are some other tips when using Optical Margin Alignment:

- ▸ Optical Margin Alignment can help to optically align centered lines that begin or end with one or more of minimal characters such as hyphens, dashes, and commas.
- ▸ When using this feature on a bulleted list, the bullets will be moved, or "hung," into the margin—a look you might or might not like. If you don't, you can turn it off for the bulleted list only.
- ▸ To choose this feature as the default for new documents, turn on Optical Margin Alignment when InDesign is running but no documents are open.
- ▸ When using InDesign's Paragraph Styles, Optical Margin Alignment can be selected or ignored. Go to Paragraph Styles Options > Indents and Spacing > Alignment > Ignore Optical Margin.

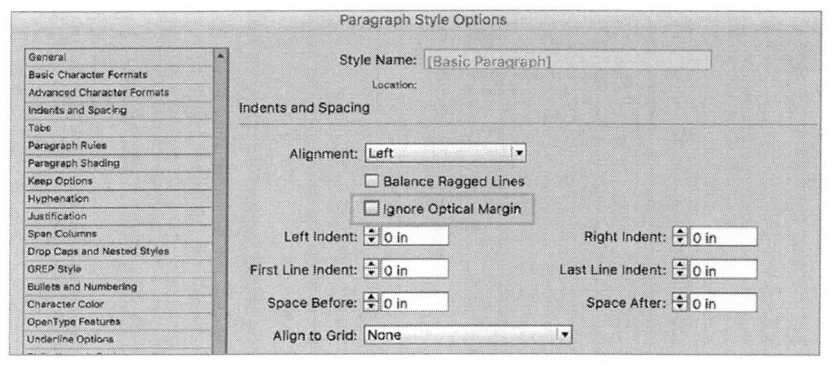

When using paragraph styles in InDesign, you can ignore Optical Margin Alignment as desired.

10

Creative Indents

While the two most common ways for handling paragraph separations are with the traditional first-line indent or a line space (not both at the same time, please!), there are other options that can add visual interest to your layout:

Extreme indent. Set the first line, or two or three lines, deeper than the usual amount—even as much as half your column width. This striking look is most effective with a wider-than-average column.

> **T**hey were indeed a queer-looking party that assembled on the bank—the birds with draggled feathers, the animals with their fur clinging close to them, and all dripping wet, cross and uncomfortable.
> The first question, of course, was how to get dry again. They had a consultation about this and after a few minutes, it seemed quite natural to Alice to find herself talking familiarly with them, as if she had known them all her life.
> At last the Mouse, who seemed to be a person of some authority among them, called out, "Sit down, all of you, and listen to me! I'll soon make you dry enough!" They all sat down at once, in a large ring, with the Mouse in the middle.

An example of extreme indents set in Expo Sans Pro with an initial set in Hobo. Text from Alice's Adventures in Wonderland, by Lewis Carroll.

CREATIVE INDENTS

Outdent. This is the opposite of an indent in that the first line hangs outside of the left margin. While it can be a very dramatic treatment, it does reduce the amount of copy that can fit in a measure.

> **T**hey were indeed a queer-looking party that assembled on
>   the bank – the birds with draggled feathers, the
>   animals with their fur clinging close to them,
>   and all dripping wet, cross and uncomfortable.
> The first question, of course, was how to get dry again. They
>   had a consultation about this and after a few
>   minutes, it seemed quite natural to Alice to
>   find herself talking familiarly with them, as if
>   she had known them all her life.
> At last the Mouse, who seemed to be a person of some authority
>   among them, called out, "Sit down, all of you,
>   and listen to me! I'll soon make you dry
>   enough!" They all sat down at once, in a large
>   ring, with the Mouse in the middle.

The same copy and setting with outdents separating the paragraphs.

Dingbat. For something a little more illustrative, try adding a dingbat or other simple graphic element between paragraphs. You can even add color. You can do this in two ways: Run the paragraphs together and separate them with a single dingbat, or use three or five centered dingbats between paragraphs separated by a line space. In either treatment, the size of the dingbat as well as the space around it are essential to a successful treatment.

> They were indeed a queer-looking party that assembled on the bank – the birds with draggled feathers, the animals with their fur clinging close to them, and all dripping wet, cross and uncomfortable. ♠ The first question, of course, was how to get dry again. They had a consultation about this and after a few minutes, it seemed quite natural to Alice to find herself talking familiarly with them, as if she had known them all her life. ♠ At last the Mouse, who seemed to be a person of some authority among them, called out, "Sit down, all of you, and listen to me! I'll soon make you dry enough!" They all sat down at once, in a large ring, with the Mouse in the middle.

Zapf Dingbats separate the paragraphs in this example. A touch of red adds to the effectiveness of this technique.

Let your creativity be your guide when designing indents, as long as they're appropriate to your content and overall design.

11

Point Size and Letter Spacing

The overall letter spacing of type should change as its size gets larger or smaller. Here's why.

The process of scaling type alters its appearance—not just in size (obviously) but in its design characteristics as well as in overall letter- and word spacing. As type gets larger (especially typefaces intended for text), thins get thicker, design details appear clunkier, and the overall spacing looks too open. Conversely, as display type is set smaller, thin strokes and fine serifs begin to get very light and disappear, design details intended to be visible at larger sizes get lost, and the overall spacing starts to look too tight.

In the days of metal type, when each point size was cut individually, minute adjustments were made to both the design and the spacing of each point size to compensate for this occurrence. But in today's world of digital type, a font consists of one scalable outline that is used for all sizes.

To compensate for this optical illusion, use your software's tracking feature to make gradual adjustments in the overall letter spacing as necessary to create an even texture. When setting display type, you may need to make some kerning adjustments to combinations that might have looked fine at small sizes but that appear too open at larger sizes.

One way that some foundries are trying to address this issue is by producing fonts that are available in optical sizes.

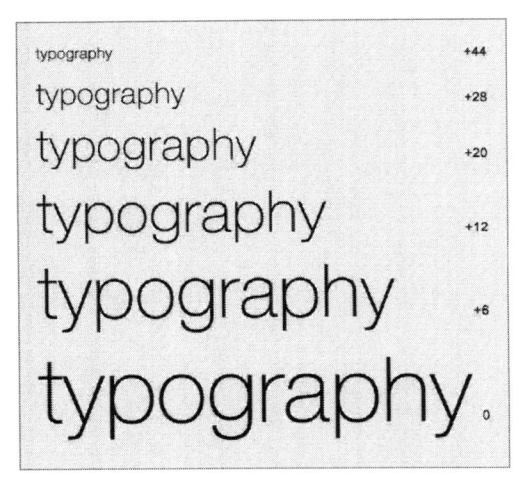

```
typography                                    +44
typography                                    +28
typography                                    +20
typography                                    +12
typography                                    +6
typography.                                    0
```

The Helvetica Neue Thin font is spaced for display usage, so when you use it at smaller point sizes, increase the tracking gradually to create the appearance of even letter spacing. In this example, the tracking for point sizes ranging from 14 to 86 point goes from +44 for the smallest size to zero for the largest in order to create optimum readability and even typographic color. (Note that the 14 point is difficult to accurately see on screen.)

POINT SIZE AND LETTER SPACING

> Typography
>
> # Typography
> # Typography

ITC Berkeley Oldstyle, a text typeface, looks fine at 12 point in print (top). But when used at a much larger size, it looks too open (middle). Reducing the tracking to –30 and adding some kern pairs makes for a much-improved appearance (bottom).

12

Kerning Principles

Q. Kerning is a black art I have yet to get my head around. How much is too much? Is it purely visual or can it be mathematical?

A: Kerning is the adjustment of space between two specific characters. While there are usually hundreds of kern pairs built into a font, sometimes you have to make manual kern adjustments—mostly to display type—to balance out the negative spaces between some letter combinations. In this regard, kerning relies on the mathematical input of font designers but may also need your "eye" to get it just right.

The goal of kerning, as well as of proper letterfit in general, is to create even color, texture, and balance between all characters. All character pairs should theoretically have the same negative space between them.

Another way to look at it is to imagine pouring sand between each pair of characters: Every space should have roughly the same volume of sand. This might sound simple, but in reality, it can be difficult to achieve due to the idiosyncrasies of the individual characters. So in answer to your question, it is a combination of mathematical and visual.

KERNING PRINCIPLES

Here are five basic principles to keep in mind when kerning.

Let Character Shapes Guide You

Proper kerning begins with understanding the spatial relationship between straight-sided characters, such as an L, and rounded characters, such as an O.

The distance between two straight characters begins with one value.

The distance between a straight and a round character (or vice versa) should be *slightly* less than two straights in order to visually look similar.

The distance between two rounds is *slightly less* than a straight and a round for the same reason.

The operative word here is "slightly," as round-to-rounds are often over-kerned by people unfamiliar with proper kerning principles (or with an untrained eye). Note that some characters are a combination of straight and round, such as b, d, g, p, and q.

ll lo ol oo

Note the relationship between the space of straight and rounded characters: straight to straights are one distance, straight to rounds (and vice versa) are slightly less, and round to rounds are slightly less than that. Set in ITC Franklin Pro.

Similar Letterforms Should Have Similar Spacing

Round to a straight character in a specific setting, such as "or," should have the same spacing as a straight to a round, such as "le."

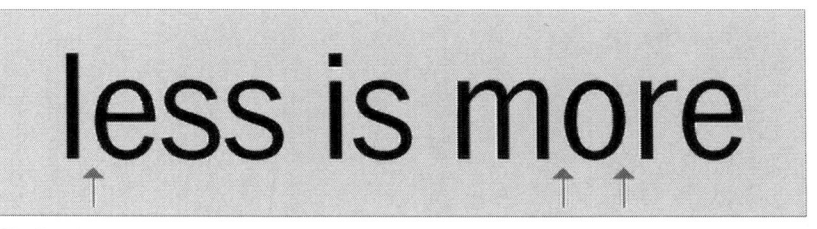

less is more

Similar letterforms, such as le, mo, and or, should have the same space between them. Set in ITC Franklin Narrow Pro.

Characters Should Rarely Touch

Straight-sided characters with serifs should not touch each other. (Neither should rounds, for that matter.) Diagonals can touch or overlap slightly, as well as some other combinations whose shapes create large negative spaces when paired with certain other characters in some fonts (such as Ty, Pr, and ry) but it's a question of taste, not a hard and fast rule.

KERNING PRINCIPLES

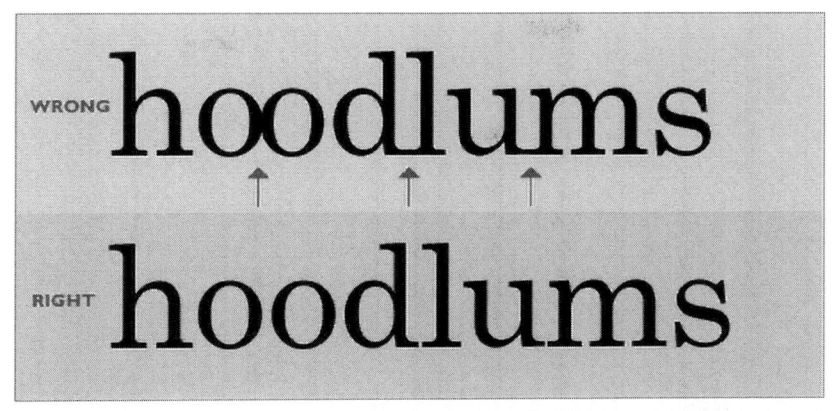

WRONG hoodlums

RIGHT hoodlums

Straight characters with serifs shouldn't touch each other (top). Neither should rounds to rounds. The lower image illustrates the proper relationships. Set in Century.

Use a Light Hand

Don't over-kern. "Less is more" when it comes to proper kerning. When in doubt, go without... kerning, that is.

Be Consistent

Consistency is critical! When kerning, review your work often to make sure you maintain consistent negative spaces, especially between the same or similar characters.

TYPETALK VOLUME 1

THE NEW VIEW

The two EW combinations are spaced differently in this example of inconsistent kerning. They should look exactly the same. Set in Gloucester MT Extra Condensed.

    You can train your eye to see spacing more acutely by observing character shapes and their spacing all around you—subway posters, magazines, book covers, packaging, menus, logos, you get the idea. Just as musicians practice their instruments, or athletes practice their sport, looking at your surroundings with a critical eye will help you to see spatial relationships that you have trouble seeing now, which in turn will help you to properly kern your typography.

13

The Ins and Outs of Tracking

The term tracking is relatively new, being a product of the digital age, and refers to a feature of today's design software related to letterspacing. It specifically pertains to the uniform opening or closing of the horizontal space between a range (more than two) of characters, whether it be a headline, caption, or an entire text setting. You can adjusting letterspacing in small increments with the tracking feature to achieve subtle, gradual refinements which can help create more readable, balanced color and texture of text. You can also use tracking to create an airy, spread-out effect. Tracking is often confused with kerning, which refers to the opening or closing of the space between two characters, and not a range.

Although a very useful function, tracking is one that is either confusing or unknown to many who use design or production software, as well as web designers who now also have access to this feature with current coding. Therefore, I will attempt to demystify this function, and explain the most common uses for it in typesetting and good design.

READABILITY
READABILITY
READABILITY

Three examples of tracking (top to bottom): 0, +100, and −50.

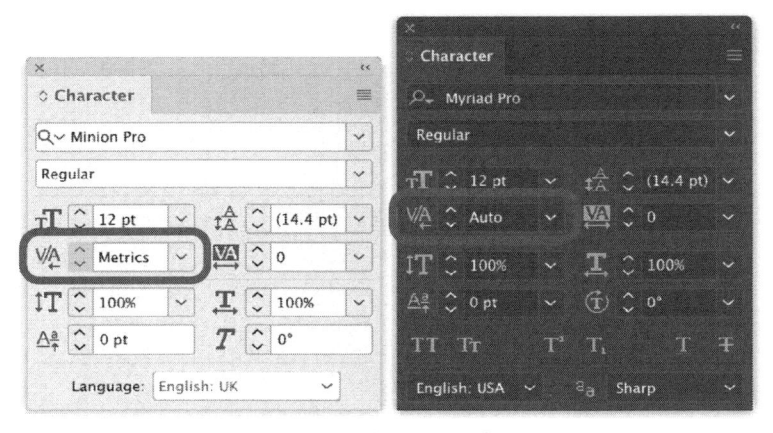

The Tracking features of InDesign (left) and Illustrator (right) are located on the Character panel.

When and How To Use Tracking

The ability to track type is important when using digital fonts, because even though the overall space between

THE INS AND OUTS OF TRACKING

glyphs in a digital font is predetermined by the typeface designer or foundry, their "one-size-fits-all" scalable outlines and fixed spacing do not actually "fit" all sizes.

Back in the days of metal type, each and every size of a given typeface was a separate "font," so the punch cutter (the person who carves the first stage of metal type) was able to make slight adjustments to the design and spacing of each point size. This important feature, which allows the customization of every size of a font, has been all but lost with today's digital type (with the exception of optical font sizes).

The glyphs of this hot metal version of (30 point) Goudy Bold don't have a lot of added "space" to their left and right. Text versions, such as 11 point, would have more space to compensate for the optical illusion of type appearing tighter as it gets smaller.

The responsibility of making the type look good an every size now falls to the designer or production artist, rather than a highly-trained typographer. They must consider the spacing of any chosen font for every size in use, and then fine-tune the spacing with the tracking feature as necessary to achieve the most readable results. This is not a skill taught in school, but one that you can learn (if you're lucky) from someone knowledgeable and experienced in the ways of typographic refinement.

As mentioned previously, each digital font is spaced (and kerned) by its designer or foundry to look best at a particular size range. Yet type is often set at a size that is much smaller or larger than that target range. It is important to remember that as type gets larger, the spacing between glyphs will optically appear to be more open; therefore, overall spacing should become tighter in order to maintain good typographic color and texture. Conversely, as type gets smaller, the spacing will appear to be tighter, which can result in decreased readability. The smaller the type size, the more open the "actual" spacing needs to be. Therefore, if you are using a typeface within its intended size range, you might not need to adjust the spacing at all. But if the built-in spacing is not ideal for the way you use the font, try opening or closing the tracking, which will help maintain good overall color and readability.

THE INS AND OUTS OF TRACKING

Brooklyn

Williamsburg Hotel, Brooklyn, New York

Williamsburg Hotel, Brooklyn, New York

The Helvetica Neue Ultra Light font is spaced by the foundry for display use, so it looks fine with 0 tracking (top). But when used to set smaller type, such as the 30 pt. setting (middle), it can appear too tight. Opening the tracking to +40 makes it easier to read (bottom).

Williamsburg Hotel, Brooklyn, New York

Williamsburg
Williamsburg

Conversely, Scala Sans looks great at text sizes (top), but when set at much larger sizes, it appears too open (middle). Use negative tracking (-45 units in this case) to reduce the inter-letter spacing, making for more balanced, readable text (bottom).

When setting type in reverse—especially small text or type on a busy background—the type will appear tighter.

In this situation, open the tracking as needed to make it appear balanced and improve readability. Other instances where tracking might be necessary include printing on porous or slick surfaces (fabric, glass, and ceramics) that might cause the ink to spread, making the type look heavier and tighter. Also, lower resolution environments, especially newspapers, which are printed on porous newsprint, might require more open spacing to avoid unintended crashing characters. On the other hand, billboards, trade show signage, and other very large display type might call for tighter spacing, no matter what the built-in spacing of the font is.

> When setting type in reverse, especially small sizes and/or a heavy weight, as well as on a busy background, the type might appear too tight. When this is the case, open the tracking in order to make it appear balanced, and improve readability.
>
> ↓
>
> When setting type in reverse, especially small sizes and/or a heavy weight, as well as on a busy background, the type might appear too tight. When this is the case, open the tracking in order to make it appear balanced, and improve readability.

When setting small type in reverse (Helvetica Neue Bold) it can appear too tight (top). Open the tracking as needed to improve readability (bottom).

Keep in mind that when adjusting the tracking, even in very small amounts, other elements might change, such as line endings, hyphenation, rags, and total number of lines. Therefore, when changing tracking, especially for small text, review your work carefully and apply any last-minute adjustments needed to make your type look as good as possible.

14

Why Distorting Type Is a Crime

Distorting type in any way, whether it be stretching, squeezing (AKA squishing), or slanting, is a type crime of the highest degree. It distorts the proportions in a way that destroys the integrity of the letter shapes. It can also reduce legibility by creating a funhouse effect.

You can see the effects of artificially condensing a typeface in the Futura example below. The condensed version that maintains pleasing curves and the minimal stroke contrast of the regular version. The squished version fails miserably in comparison, with its ugly egg-shaped contours and exaggerated stroke contrast.

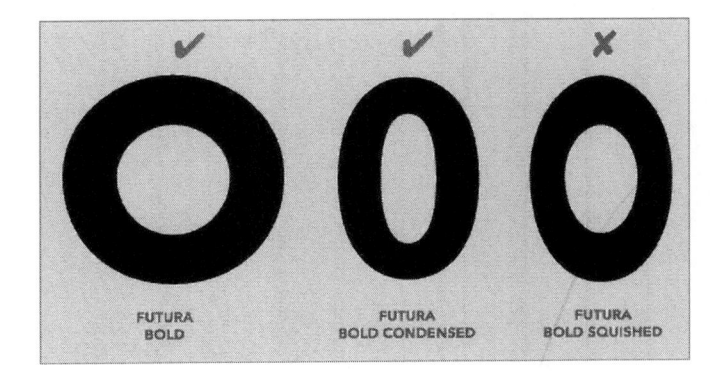

✔ FUTURA BOLD ✔ FUTURA BOLD CONDENSED ✘ FUTURA BOLD SQUISHED

Check out the difference between Futura Oblique and the computer-generated slanted version below. The fake slanted version on the right has a more distorted shape, as well as uneven and exaggerated stroke contrast.

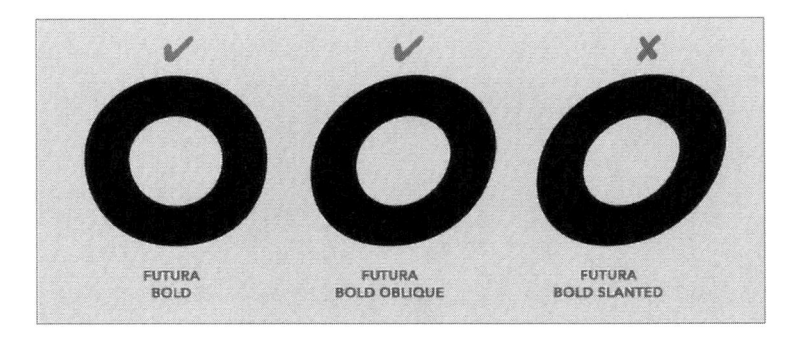

✓	✓	✗
O	O	O
FUTURA BOLD	FUTURA BOLD OBLIQUE	FUTURA BOLD SLANTED

Finally, observe the unpleasant result of stretching Univers. The true-drawn extended version, second from the left, looks far better than the two examples of computer stretching on the right.

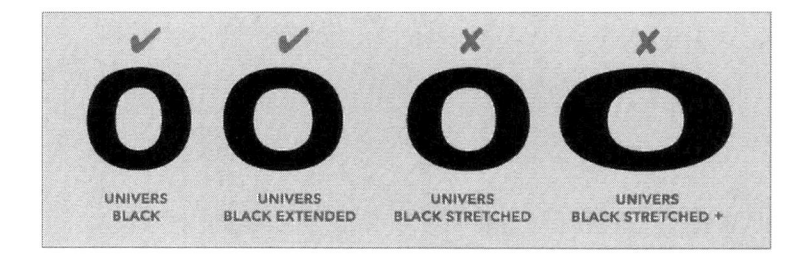

✓	✓	✗	✗
O	O	O	O
UNIVERS BLACK	UNIVERS BLACK EXTENDED	UNIVERS BLACK STRETCHED	UNIVERS BLACK STRETCHED +

A way to avoid these requests for artificial distortions is to pick a typeface or type family that contains legitimate, true-drawn width variants. When created by a skillful type designer, a width variant maintains the weight contrast between thick and thin; the relationships of the horizontals and verticals; the axis of the character stress of italics (when applicable); the thickness and integrity of

WHY DISTORTING TYPE IS A CRIME

the serifs, if any; the overall width of character; and the spacing.

Don't give in to these requests to "set to fit" or fill in white space! Instead, work with the chosen typefaces and other elements to make a successful composition and overall design.

15

Glyph Positioning and Baseline Shift

Glyph positioning is a topic that addresses one of the small yet important typographic details that goes unnoticed by most, but is appreciated by the typographic savvy.

Glyph positioning refers to the raising or lowering of certain punctuation and symbols, such as hyphens, dashes, and parentheses, to make them optically centered, or positioned according to the designer's or clients needs. So why should you be concerned about this? Here's why: The vertical placement of these characters, and all other glyphs in any given font, is determined by the typeface designer based on what kind of characters they most often appear next to (for example, caps vs. lowercase). But in some instances where these glyphs are very noticeable, the vertical placement calls for a bit of adjusting. I'm not talking about running text where tweaking small details would be much too tedious and time-consuming, but those glyphs that stand out, such as those in headlines and subheads, book and magazine covers, signage, business cards, and resumes.

The ability to raise or lower any glyph can be achieved with the Baseline Shift function found in Adobe InDesign

GLYPH POSITIONING AND BASELINE SHIFT

and Illustrator as well as in other software with robust typographic features. Here's how:

1. Select the glyph with the Type tool
2. Go to the Control Panel or Character panel
3. Locate the Baseline Shift field
4. Click on the Up or Down arrow key, or
5. Type a numeric value (including fractional values) in the Baseline Shift field. Positive values raise the text; negative values lower the text.

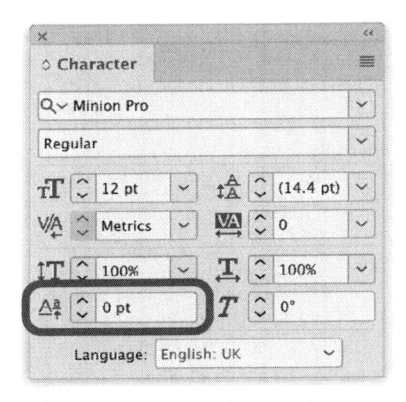

InDesign's Glyph Positioning feature is located on the bottom left of the Character Panel. Be sure to have Show Options activated in the panel menu.

Note: Baseline Shift does not change the actual line spacing of a character, so when making overall changes in the leading, the baseline-shifted position will be preserved proportionally.

The sections below call out those glyphs that most commonly call for vertical adjusting.

Hyphens

Hyphens are customarily positioned slightly above the center of a font's x-height. This works well for running copy as well as oldstyle figures. But when used with (or next to) cap-height glyphs or lining figures, the hyphens appear too low. When this is the case, raise them slightly to the optical center or to the desired position.

-x-—X -x-—X
-x--X -x-—X
-x-—X -x-—X

The vertical position of hyphens and dashes in most fonts is centered on the x-height, and might need to be adjusted when they appear next to cap-height glyphs.

273-845-2145
273-845-2145
VICE-PRESIDENT
VICE-PRESIDENT

Two examples of raising the hyphen for a more centered appearance next to lining figures and caps. (Font default locations in red.)

GLYPH POSITIONING AND BASELINE SHIFT

En and em dashes

Dashes are also (usually) positioned to look good next to lowercase. When used next to cap height glyphs, such as caps and lining figures, they might need to be raised.

> *—The Winston News*
> *—The Winston News*

Em dashes next to captials should be raised so they don't appear too low.

Parentheses, braces, and brackets

The parenthesis, brace, and brackets in a font are commonly positioned to center around the lowercase. But when used to enclose all caps or lining figures, they will look too low. Raising them to center around the type they enclose makes for a more balanced setting.

> **New York City (NYC)**
> **New York City (NYC)**
> **(nyc)**

Brackets might need to be raised when enclosing all caps.

Trademark (™) and Registered Trademark (®) symbols

Trademark symbols frequently call for adjusting their vertical position to place them exactly where you want them in relation to the glyph they follow. Baseline shift is perfect for this! If they need to be resized, do this before adjusting their vertical position. (Note that their size and vertical position can vary greatly from font to font.)

> # Homevisors®
> # Homevisors®

This registered symbol was reduced and then lowered and kerned for a more balanced appearance.

Quotes and apostrophes

Quotation marks and apostrophes are usually fine where they naturally appear. But on occasion, they can benefit from some tweaking of their vertical placement.

> *The southern belle's handbook*
> *The southern belle's handbook*

This apostrophe (top) was lowered and then kerned (bottom).

GLYPH POSITIONING AND BASELINE SHIFT

Bullets and other font-based graphics

Bullets (and any graphics used as markers in a bulleted list) are a common element in many kinds of text. Depending on what symbol is being used, you may have to check its vertical placement to make sure they it's optically centered next to the majority of points, or wherever you deem is the best placement. Make sure the size is right before you adjust the bullets, and make all of them the same, even if their neighboring glyphs differ.

> • reduces mold, viruses and germs
> • reduces mold, viruses and germs
> ✂ cut coupon along these lines
> ✂ cut coupon along these lines

Bullets and other font-based graphics often need to be adjusted for a more centered appearance.

All typography should look readable and inviting without being disrupted by typographic distractions, which, although seemingly insignificant, can make a huge difference in the overall appearance of your text. So if your goal is to achieve professional-looking results, review the above-mentioned details towards the end of every job, and make any necessary adjustments to finesse your typography.

16

Know Your Hyphens and Dashes

Hyphens, en dashes, and em dashes are three visually similar yet significantly different punctuation marks that commonly appear in text. Their definition and purpose are frequently misunderstood by designers and writers alike, often leading to inaccurate and unprofessional typography. While some of this confusion is a result of typewriter conventions still being used in today's digital world, it is ultimately up to the person doing the typesetting—whether a production artist, web programmer, or graphic designer—to get it right. Writers, take heed as well!

> hyphen -
> en dash –
> em dash —

The differences between all three symbols are clear in this setting of Clarendon.

KNOW YOUR HYPHENS AND DASHES

Description and usage

A hyphen (-) is the shortest in width of the three, and is used to hyphenate words that break at the end of a line, as well as to connect compound words, such as mother-in-law, well-being, and merry-go-round. It is also used for phone numbers. The hyphen is easily found to the right of the zero on most keyboards.

> *mother-in-law   well-being   merry-go-round*
> **212-345-6811**

Hyphens are used to connect many compound words as well as for phone numbers.

An en dash (–) is wider than a hyphen and narrower than an em dash, and is the most misunderstood of the three. This dash is used to indicate a range, that is, elements that are related by distance, including time, years, and dates, such as 3 pm–6 pm, Monday–Friday, March 2–7, or pages 20–55. In fact, an en dash is correct in any instance where a preposition such as the words "to" and "from" can be substituted. Commit this to memory: Press Option+hyphen on a Mac or Alt+0150 in Windows (Alt+hyphen in InDesign) to get an en dash.

TYPETALK VOLUME 1

Monday–Friday	Monday–Friday	Monday–Friday
4 PM–6 PM	4 PM–6 PM	4 PM–6 PM
March 1–30	March 1–30	March 1–30
1892–1945	1892–1945	1892–1945

The en dash, which is wider than a hyphen and narrower than an em dash, is used to indicate a range, as well as a continuation of time.

An em dash (—) is the longest of the three, and is most commonly used to indicate a break in thought, or a thought within a thought or a sentence. It is accessed by pressing Option+Shift+hyphen on a Mac and Alt+0151 in Windows (Alt+Shift+hyphen in InDesign). One of the most common type crimes associated with this symbol is the use of two hyphens instead of an em dash. This typographically incorrect practice is a holdover from typewriter days when two hyphens were used as a replacement for the dash, which didn't exist on the keyboard. Unfortunately, this is still a widespread occurrence that you can see everywhere from print to the web to movie titles and kinetic type.

KNOW YOUR HYPHENS AND DASHES

> The line had not yet been surveyed. When the Blackfeet were told that the Americans—Long Knives—owned the country to the south of the Hills, and the English—the Red Coats—the land north of them, they only laughed, and said: "That is a mistake. Neither the Red Coats nor the Long Knives own any of this country."

> The line had not yet been surveyed. When the Blackfeet were told that the Americans – Long Knives – owned the country to the south of the Hills, and the English – the Red Coats – the land north of them, they only laughed, and said: "That is a mistake. Neither the Red Coats nor the Long Knives own any of this country."

> The line had not yet been surveyed. When the Blackfeet were told that the Americans--Long Knives--owned the country to the south of the Hills, and the English--the Red Coats--the land north of them, they only laughed, and said: "That is a mistake. Neither the Red Coats nor the Long Knives own any of this country."

The standard em dash is grammatically correct for a break in thought, or a thought within a thought (upper left). But if the em dash seems too wide for a particular typeface, and/or the spacing is too tight, it can be replaced with an en dash, and the spacing opened up for either dash as desired (upper right). The use of two hyphens instead of a dash is a major type crime, and should never be used in fine typography (lower). Excerpt from *Sinopah the Indian Boy*, by James Willard Schultz.

Design differences

The length of dashes is not standard, and can vary from typeface to typeface, as does the designated space surrounding them (technically called sidebearings). Some en dashes are close to the width of the n and em dashes the width of the m, keeping them in proportion to the rest of the typeface. Others have no relationship to the overall width of the typeface at all, with some being a set 500 and 1,000 units to the em square (a measurement relative to the point size of the type), respectively. Because of this, the width and fit of dashes can vary dramatically.

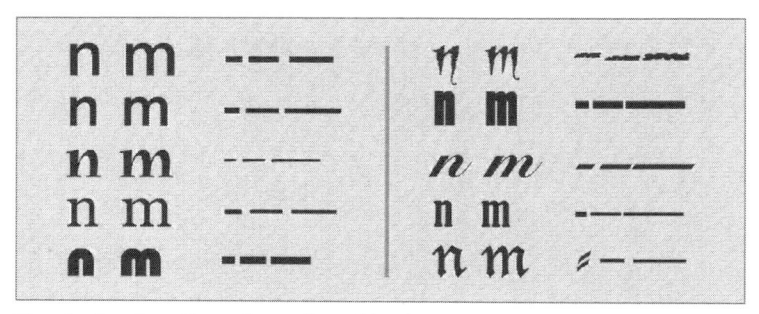

The design, length, and spacing of hyphens and en and em dashes can vary tremendously from typeface to typeface.

Finessing the details

When the width of an em dash seems out of proportion to the typeface in use (for example, it may be too wide for use in a condensed typeface), or either dash appears too close to its neighboring characters, there is room for artistic or "typographic" license to improve their appearance. For instance, when the em dash seems too wide, many typographically savvy designers will substitute an en dash, which is an accepted practice in fine typography. Additionally, when the spacing around either dash seems too tight, it can be opened up to add additional breathing room and more closely match the overall spacing of the rest of the typeface. A good way to do this is with the use

KNOW YOUR HYPHENS AND DASHES

of the kerning feature, which will give you total control over the amount of space added. Another solution is to add a word space on both ends, which is the recommended practice on the web, but more of a personal preference in print. Just remember to be consistent in your treatment throughout, or the text can become an unprofessional jumble of varying styles.

17

The Definitive Guide to Quotes, Apostrophes, and Primes

Quotation marks, apostrophes, and primes (also known as inch and foot marks) are some of the most misunderstood and misused elements in typesetting. The confusion between them hearkens back to the days of typewriters, when there was just one style—now called 'typewriter quotes'—to represent them all. But today's computers are intended to set professional typography, not just provide typing for the casual user; therefore the proper glyphs are available in most fonts. Understanding the distinction between these marks and the task of getting them right can be challenging, but essential, for the creative professional.

If you think you've heard me ranting about this topic before, you are right. That is because the misuse of any of these glyphs is one of the most widespread of all type crimes in digital typography, committed by students and novices (who have an excuse) and seasoned professionals (who don't). This can be due to lack of knowledge, but also because too many creative professionals don't think it is their job to be concerned about this. They are wrong, as every design job is a group effort, and any error reflects poorly on the entire team, and most especially, the client.

THE DEFINITIVE GUIDE TO QUOTES, APOSTROPHES, AND PRIMES

So ranting aside, here is all you need to know to be on the right side of the law—typographically speaking!

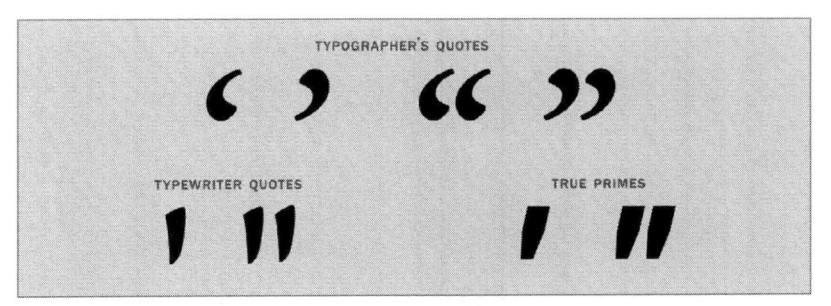

TYPOGRAPHER'S QUOTES
' ' " "

TYPEWRITER QUOTES
' "

TRUE PRIMES
′ ″

There are distinct differences between 'smart' typographer's quotes, 'dumb' typewriter quotes, and true primes. Set in Arno Pro.

Quotation marks, also referred to as smart quotes, typographer's quotes, and sometimes curly quotes (although they don't have to be truly curly) are used to set off a word, passage, or group of sentences. They have an open (or left) and a closed (or right) version, and are design-sensitive, meaning they look different for each typeface, as they are intended to match, or blend, with each design.

Apostrophes are used to indicate possession and omission. The actual glyph used for an apostrophe in typesetting is the closed (or right) single quote—not a typewriter quote, or an open single quote (which frequently appears by default when typing, as software is not yet smart enough to know the difference in usage). A good way to determine if the correct glyph is being used is to compare it to a comma, because in most fonts, the comma is the same design as the true quote.

Primes, more commonly referred to as inch and foot marks, are different from quotation marks in that they are more neutral in appearance (as opposed to matching each typeface). True primes are actually slightly angled, tapered marks, but are not available in very many fonts. For this reason, the glyphs most often used to set measurements are the typewriter quotes (also called straight or dumb quotes) available in just about all fonts. A select few OpenType fonts have true primes, either instead of the old-fashioned typewriter quotes or in addition to them. When available, true primes should be used for measurements, but typewriter quotes have become the accepted practice in digital typography.

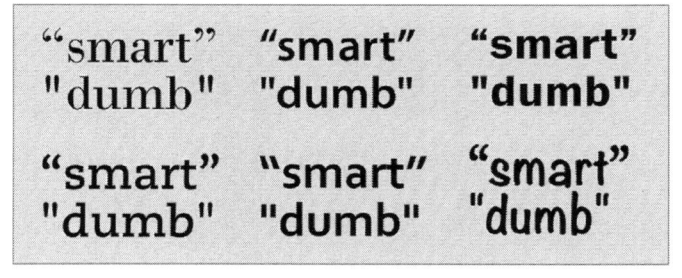

"smart" "smart" "smart"
"dumb" "dumb" "dumb"

"smart" "smart" "smart"
"dumb" "dumb" "dumb"

Smart quotes are design-sensitive glyphs, compared to the relatively simple design of "dumb" or typewriter quotes.

Getting it right!

Misuse of quotes and primes is one of the most common typographic errors in professional typesetting and can be found everywhere from ads, brochures, book covers, magazines, and newspapers, to websites and blogs, movie titles, motion graphics, and other digital media.

THE DEFINITIVE GUIDE TO QUOTES, APOSTROPHES, AND PRIMES

Why is this type crime so prevalent? Because the standard computer keyboard layout is based on the typewriter keyboard with its old-fashioned straight quotes serving double duty, and designers and software manufacturers are left to straighten out the mess!

The proper use of quotes and primes should also be applied to the web and all digital media, if possible. In some instances, smart quotes have to be manually coded, while other scenarios allow for automatic conversion. Unfortunately, there are some environments that do not support the use of smart quotes—or the use of both smart and dumb quotes—at all, or make it too tedious to implement on a large scale. These include some content management systems (commonly referred to as CMSs) as well as some email marketing systems, so do your research carefully before you buy into one of these systems.

There are some situations where errors might automatically occur. One is when you use any method to globally convert dumb quotes to smart quotes, in which case measurements will also be converted. For that reason, be sure to proofread all final copy, and convert back any incorrect smart quotes to primes, or dumb, typewriter quotes. The other potential situation is in words that use apostrophes for omissions. The default glyph in front of any character will be the open single quote, but for omissions (such as the '90s or rock 'n roll), the only correct glyph is the apostrophe, which is a closed, single quote. Check carefully for these errors, and change them back manually.

> My "new" office is 10' × 12'4"
> My "new" office is 10' × 12'4"

> 'Tis but a scratch!
> 'Tis but a scratch!
>
> rock 'n' roll
> rock 'n' roll

Always check for the correct usage of quotes and measurement glyphs. The circled punctuation is incorrect.

Here are some tips to help get it right.

The first step is to make sure the original copy contains typographically correct punctuation. One way to help accomplish this is to change the default setting in Microsoft Word's Autocorrect preferences from "straight quotations marks" to "smart quotations marks." Suggest this practice to all who submit final copy. Note that when typing directly into design software, this is less of a problem, as the default setting of most design apps is to automatically use typographer's quotes when typing.

THE DEFINITIVE GUIDE TO QUOTES, APOSTROPHES, AND PRIMES

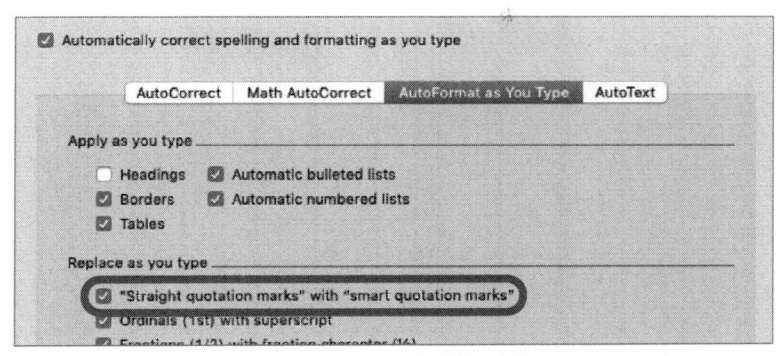

Changing the default punctuation of Microsoft Word to automatically change straight quotes to smart quotes will minimize the work you have to do later to correct them.

If you're working with a document with incorrect punctuation and want to clean it up before insertion, use a utility such as Tex-Edit Plus that can clean up a document to your specifications in seconds.

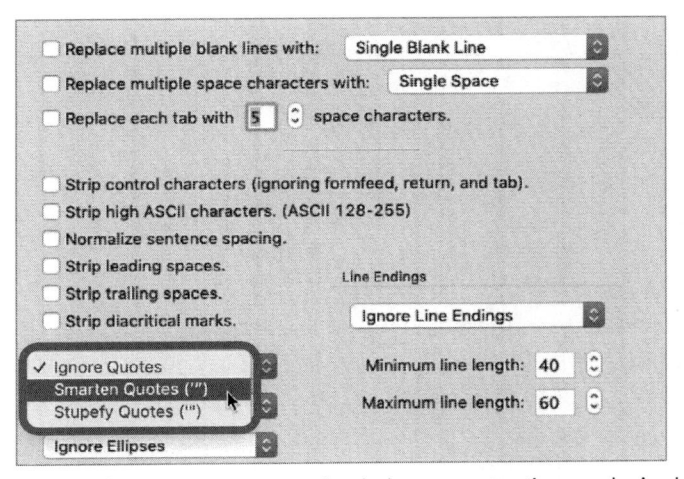

Tex-Edit Plus can smarten or dumb down punctuation, as desired.

For a long-term solution, create a guide of best practices that includes all required typographic conventions, including the use of smart quotes. Distribute the guidelines to all the writers, editors, copyeditors, proofreaders, designers, webmasters, and programmers so that everyone is on the same page, so to speak.

When preparing or submitting copy for digital use, call out the appearance of quotes and primes so the programmer or developer can do whatever necessary to get it right.

Import text properly, using the Place command available in most design software. When using InDesign, select Show Import Options, and choose the option to Use Typographer's Quotes towards the bottom. Review imported text, and make sure all measurement are set with primes and omissions are set with proper apostrophes.

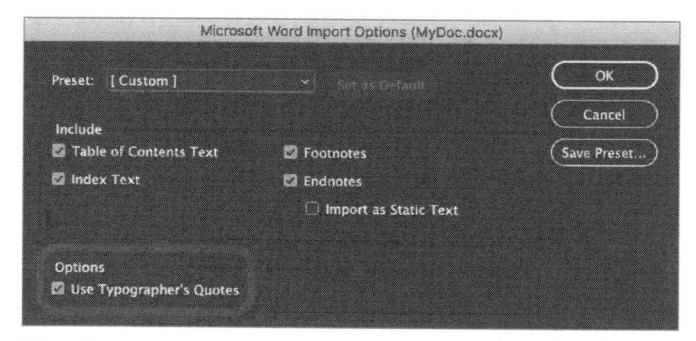

When importing text into InDesign using Place, select Import Options that allow for the automatic conversion to typographer's quotes. When importing a Word document, the appropriate dialog box will appear, as shown above.

THE DEFINITIVE GUIDE TO QUOTES, APOSTROPHES, AND PRIMES

If you are using copy from an email, a PDF, or the web, make sure the punctuation is corrected before you copy and paste. (Here is where Tex-Exit Plus comes in handy.)

Check for the correct use of apostrophes (and not open single quotes) in contractions and omissions.

At the risk of sounding like a broken record, always proofread your work carefully to check for these important type crimes. The more eyes that review final copy, the better.

18

Finessing the Details of Type: Trademark and Copyright Symbols

Every designer and typesetter at one time or another needs to use one or more of these three symbols: trademark, registered trademark, and copyright. What might seem like a tiny legal detail needs to be typeset thoughtfully in order to be legible, readable, and not draw undue attention to itself. If you just accept the default symbol in the font without paying attention to its size, design, and placement, you can wind up with either a huge, distracting symbol, or a tiny, unreadable one that looks like a smudge. Here are some tips for finessing these tiny yet important details.

Registered Trademark and Trademark symbols (® and ™)

The registered and trademark symbols vary from one typeface to another. Some are related in design to the overall typeface, and others, not so much. These symbols are used at so small a size that they should be neutral in appearance, yet clear at the size they will be reproduced at. If their design is too stylized, hard to read, or just plain ugly, you can substitute the symbol from another font for all instances. For text usages, Uncomplicated sans serif

FINESSING THE DETAILS OF TYPE: TRADEMARK AND COPYRIGHT SYMBOLS

symbols (such as those from Helvetica, Arial, or Franklin Gothic) are a good choice, as they tend to be very readable and print cleanly and clearly at small sizes. When setting a headline, you have more latitude with respect to the design, as readability is less of a problem.

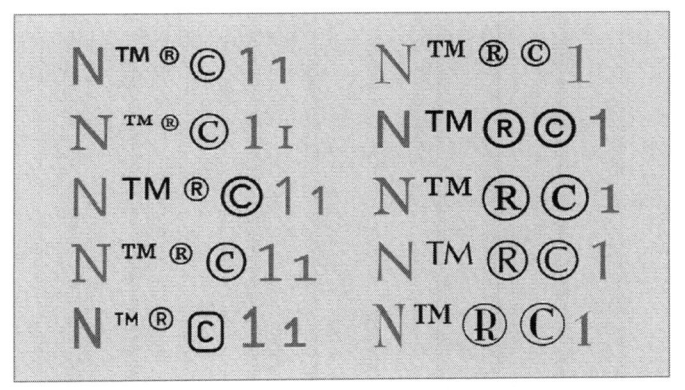

These three symbols, shown between a cap and two styles of figures when available, vary in size and design from font to font. The ones on the left have the correct relationship to the caps and lowercase, while the ones on the right are either too small (top, copyright symbol) or too large (lower, trademark and registered trademark symbols).

Some font families that have been updated, such as Avenir and Avenir Next will adjust the scale of these symbols to more closely resemble their intended usage.

Size is important as well, especially since these symbols vary so much in scale from font to font. Therefore, when using a ® or a ™ after a word, the size should be adjusted as necessary, independently from the rest of the text, to look clear and legible, yet unobtrusive. A general guideline for text is to make these symbols a little smaller than half the x-height of the adjacent text. As the type gets larger, the symbols can become proportionately smaller, especially in headlines. These symbols are legal designations, not exciting graphic elements, and making them too large can detract from the overall design.

Spacing, both horizontal and vertical in relation to the neighboring glyph, will then have to be evaluated. Once the glyphs are sized appropriately, you will most likely have to adjust the letter spacing (using kerning) as well as the vertical position (using baseline shift).

Springfield Gardens®
Springfield Gardens®
Springfield Gardens®
Gardens®
Gardens®

A general guideline for text is to make these symbols a little smaller than half the x-height. As the text gets larger, they should become proportionately smaller, especially when used in headlines. Set in Expo Sans.

FINESSING THE DETAILS OF TYPE: TRADEMARK AND COPYRIGHT SYMBOLS

Springfield Gardens™
Springfield Gardens™

Springfield Gardens™
Springfield Gardens™

Gardens™
Gardens™

Some symbols in serif fonts might not only appear too large, but their thin strokes can start to disappear at small sizes. It is always an option to use one from a sans serif font, such as the examples in black. Set in Cochin.

Copyright symbol (©)

Unlike the registered and trademark symbols, the copyright symbol is most often typeset to more closely match the size of the cap height, which also works for most (but not all) figures. This glyph can usually be used just as it appears in the font, with little or no adjustment. But if it appears before a shorter oldstyle figure (such as an oldstyle 1 as in 1973) or an x-height glyph, it can be reduced a bit if it seems too large. Once it's sized the way you want it, check the horizontal spacing as well as the vertical position, and adjust with kerning and baseline shift as desired.

©1989 Sergenta Cove
©1989 Sergenta Cove
©1989 Sergenta Cove

The copyright symbol in this font is too small (top). Enlarging it and adjusting the vertical and horizontal spacing is an improvement, but now the circle looks too heavy (middle). The typography gods are appeased when a symbol from another font is substituted (lower).

©1989 Sergenta Cove
©1989 Sergenta Cove

The copyright symbol in this example (set in French Script) is too high when used next to figures, which are shorter than the caps. Lowering it to center on the figures makes it more balanced.

©1989 Sergenta Cove
©1989 Sergenta Cove
©1989 Sergenta Cove

These three examples, set in Alfon Bold, are all appropriate: the copyright symbol from each font looks good next to lining figures, oldstyle figures, and italic figures. Note that the symbol is, correctly, not italicized in the third example.

FINESSING THE DETAILS OF TYPE: TRADEMARK AND COPYRIGHT SYMBOLS

Paying close attention to these common legal symbols will contribute to the overall professionalism of your work. But keep in mind the client's specs can supersede the designer's aesthetics.

19

Choosing and Using Swash Characters

Want to enhance and spiff up an otherwise ordinary or lackluster type treatment? Try using swash characters. A swash is a flourish or stroke extension that is attached to a glyph for purely decorative purposes. They most commonly appear at the beginning or end of a glyph (usually referred to as initial and terminal swashes), but they can also be found attached to ascenders and descenders, crossbars, and glyph apexes.

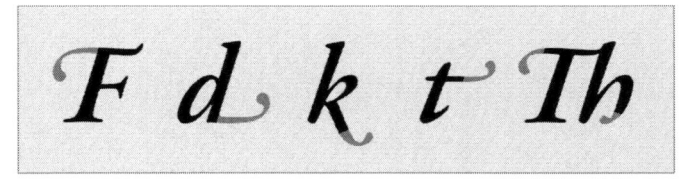

F d k t Th

A variety of swash types found in Adobe Garamond Premier are shown in orange.

The incorporation of swash characters into a setting is a great way to draw attention to and embellish type. They are commonly used in invitations, logos and product branding, packaging, movie titles, book covers, magazines, websites…you get the idea. They are also a terrific option for initial letters. Swashes can be used to add an air of panache, elegance, or importance to a type treatment.

CHOOSING AND USING SWASH CHARACTERS

The tasteful use of swash characters can help you avoid overusing repeated forms and can make a setting look more like a custom, hand-lettered composition.

You might assume that swash characters are available only in fancy script typefaces, but actually, they can occur in both serif and sans designs, text and display faces, formal, informal and casual scripts, and even handwriting fonts. In fact, they are said to have evolved from decorative handwriting many centuries ago. Some fonts contain swashes for caps only, and others only in the italic versions. (ITC Zapf Chancery Medium Italic is an example of the latter, as the upright medium weight is unadorned.) Swashes can also be found in ligatures, such as Th. While they are usually optional glyphs, some fonts use decorative swashes as the standard characters, and (might) contain the otherwise simple versions as alternates.

Antarctica
INITIAL SWASH

Antarctica
TERMINAL SWASH

Initial swashes should only be used at the beginning of a line or word, while terminal swashes work best at the end of a line or word.

PF Champion Script has hundreds of swash characters and flourishes, so designing with them requires lots of trial and error to get just the right look.

Centaur is an historic typeface that contains some rather conservative swashes and companion flourishes that can dress up an otherwise unremarkable setting.

CHOOSING AND USING SWASH CHARACTERS

Wildwood Falls

Wildwood Falls

The addition of swashes in this sans serif typeface gives a fun vibe to this logo. Set in Wedding Singer.

Caprizant

Beloved Script

Ed's Market Upright Script

Some might call Laura Worthington the queen of swashes. She has designed hundreds of typefaces with swashes, including these three.

TYPETALK VOLUME 1

> *E*mma Woodhouse, handsome, clever, and rich, with a comfortable home and happy disposition, seemed to unite some of the best blessings of existence; and had lived nearly twenty-one years in the world with very little to distress or vex her. She was the youngest of the two daughters of a most affectionate, indulgent father; and had, in consequence of her sister's marriage, been mistress of his house from a very early period.

This swash *E* set in ITC Bodoni SeventyTwo Italic makes a lovely initial character when used with its companion text, ITC Bodoni Six. Excerpt from *Emma*, by Jane Austen.

How to find and apply swash characters in InDesign

The increasing availability of swash characters in fonts is primarily due to the extended character set of today's font format of choice, OpenType. OpenType fonts have space for many additional characters—thousands, actually! The challenge is to find out whether any particular font—whether it be in your current font library or one you are considering purchasing—has swash characters. This can sometimes be challenging, since not only do fonts differ in how they categorize swashes, but design software differs in how to locate and apply them.

Swash characters are usually classified and identified as a Swash in design software, and they can be found as such in InDesign's Glyphs panel. But in some fonts they are classified as Stylistic or Contextual Alternates. Swashes can be accessed in two ways: either globally by

CHOOSING AND USING SWASH CHARACTERS

choosing OpenType from the Character or Control panel menu, or individually from the Glyphs panel. If applied globally to any selected text, all available swashes in the font will replace the standard glyphs. While this is the fastest and easiest way to apply them, if the font in question has numerous swash characters, you might end up with too many in a given setting. When this is the case, you're better off using the Glyphs panel. That way you have total control over the appearance of your type.

The swash characters in Adobe Garamond Premier are found under the Swash and Stylistic Alternate categories in the Glyph panel.

TYPETALK VOLUME 1

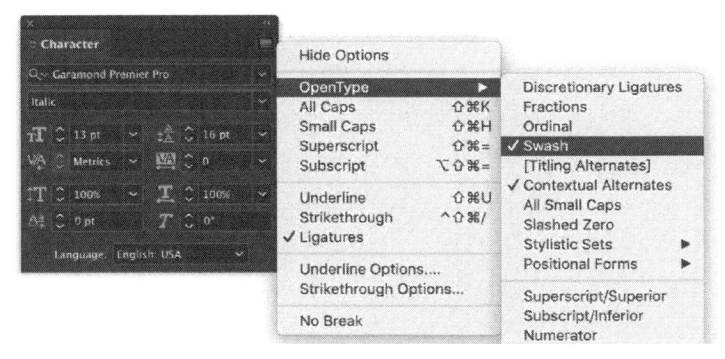

Swashes can be turned on globally via InDesign's Character panel.

When using a font with many swash characters, don't make the mistake of applying them globally, or you might get a hot mess such as this (upper right). Take the time to insert just the ones you want individually from the Glyphs panel for a tasteful result (bottom).

CHOOSING AND USING SWASH CHARACTERS

Please, do us all a favor: Don't use swash characters in all-cap settings. They are almost impossible to read when set one next to the other, as they were not intended—both in design and spacing—to be used this way.

Swashes and Glyph Substitution

OpenType fonts have a feature called glyph substitution. This capability is a built-in script, or brain, in a manner of speaking, that programs a font to know when to insert situational glyphs, which can include initial, medial, and terminal swashes as well as alternates. This is an optional feature that has to be programmed into the font. Unfortunately, there is usually no way to know in advance (unless the foundry indicates this) if a font has this built-in brain, except by trial and error. It can be an extremely useful and time-saving feature for a font that contains many or location-specific swashes. For instance, some swash characters are intended for either the beginning or end of a word to avoid crashing into other letters or creating too much space between two characters. When a font has glyph substitution, the correct swash will be automatically inserted. If the copy is changed, it will automatically change the swash character back to the standard one as necessary. (You (the user) can always override this.)

TYPETALK VOLUME 1

interpretation

interpretation

interpretations

misinterpretation

Glyph substitution is built into PF Champion Script, making the insertion of the correct swash happen automatically as you type, as long as you have Contextual Alternates turned on (as it was below the top setting). Swashes will appear at the beginning and ending of the word, and will adjust as you add or delete characters. Note the swash characters in this font are identified as Stylistic or Contextual Alternates, not swashes.

While swashes can be a wonderful enhancement to a type setting, not all swashes are well-designed and created with useful purpose. Mark Jamra of TypeCulture has designed swash caps for three of his classically-inspired typefaces: Expo Serif Pro, Jamille Pro, and Latienne Pro. In his typical witty yet observant manner, he says that "there are three kinds of swashes: really well-conceived swashes that make a typographic contribution, OK swashes that someone might use somewhere,

CHOOSING AND USING SWASH CHARACTERS

and completely pointless swashes that are only useful for marketing the font." Whether you agree with him or not (and I do!), it makes sense to explore the fonts with swash characters you might have in your own library, as well as those in fonts you are considering using. Keep in mind that they should be used sparingly and thoughtfully so they don't overwhelm and overpower. When used tastefully and appropriately, they can make the difference between a just "OK" design and one that stands out from the crowd.

The Legend *of* Zorro → *The* **L**egend *of* **Z**ORRO

The use of the swashes as well as true-drawn small caps which are available in Latienne Pro transform a simple title into a much more exciting one.

20

A Blizzard of White Space Characters

Most (if not all) design applications have a collection of white-space characters intended to help you fine-tune your work. Some of these non-printing characters are more useful than others. Here's a list to help you make sense of them.

Em Space: Equal in width to the size of the type. For instance, in 12-point type, an em space is 12 points wide.

En Space: One half the width of an em space.

Third Space or 3-per-Em-Space: One third the width of an em space.

Quarter Space or 4-per-Em-Space: One fourth the width of an em space.

Sixth Space or 6-per-Em-Space: One sixth the width of an em space.

Thin Space: One eighth the width of an em space. Often used on either side of an em or en dash (although I prefer the kern function for this).

A BLIZZARD OF WHITE SPACE CHARACTERS

Hair Space: One twenty-fourth the width of an em space.

Flush Space: Adds a variable amount of space to the last line of a fully justified paragraph, useful for justifying text in the last line.

Figure Space: Same width as a tabular numeral in the typeface. Can be used to help align numbers in financial tables.

Punctuation Space: Same width as the exclamation point, period, or colon in the typeface.

Nonbreaking Space or Word Joiner: When placed between two words, it prevents them from being broken at the end of a line. It's flexible in that it can expand or compress in justified type.

Nonbreaking Space (Fixed Width): The same as the above, but it doesn't expand or compress in justified text.

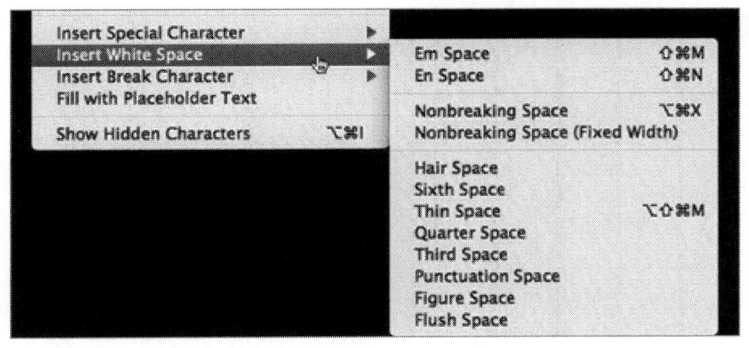

InDesign's white spaces are located in the Type > Insert White Space menu.

21

Typography for Presentations

Whether you use a presentation application such as Microsoft PowerPoint and Apple Keynote or a multi-page PDF (as I do) for your presentations, the objective is the same: Engage the audience and support the main points of the speaker's information. The goal is not to replicate your talk word-for-word, nor to present complicated charts, diagrams, detailed financials, and text-heavy slides. Succeeding in those goals would bore your audience to tears.

The following simple guidelines will help you create a presentation that will engage your audience:

- **Restrict your presentation to a maximum of two typefaces.** One for headlines and subheads, another for text. Use strong fonts with a high degree of onscreen readability. Decorative and detailed fonts are harder to read onscreen and therefore less effective.
- **Keep text large.** 20 to 24 point minimum. Small text is hard to read on a screen, especially from a distance.
- **Maximize contrast.** When choosing color(s) for the background and/or the text, make sure the

text stands out. Keep the color scheme simple and consistent.
- **Minimize clutter.** Don't place type on top of busy backgrounds or images.
- **Restrict each slide to six or fewer lines of type.** Present the highlights of your talk, not the actual text. More slides with less type are better than fewer, text-heavy slides.
- **Keep lines short.** Edit your thoughts to the fewest words possible; you can elaborate verbally.

I used one typeface, Gill Sans Pro, in different weights and versions for the body of the slides below. The contrasting colors pop, and lots of space contributes to clean, simple, readable type.

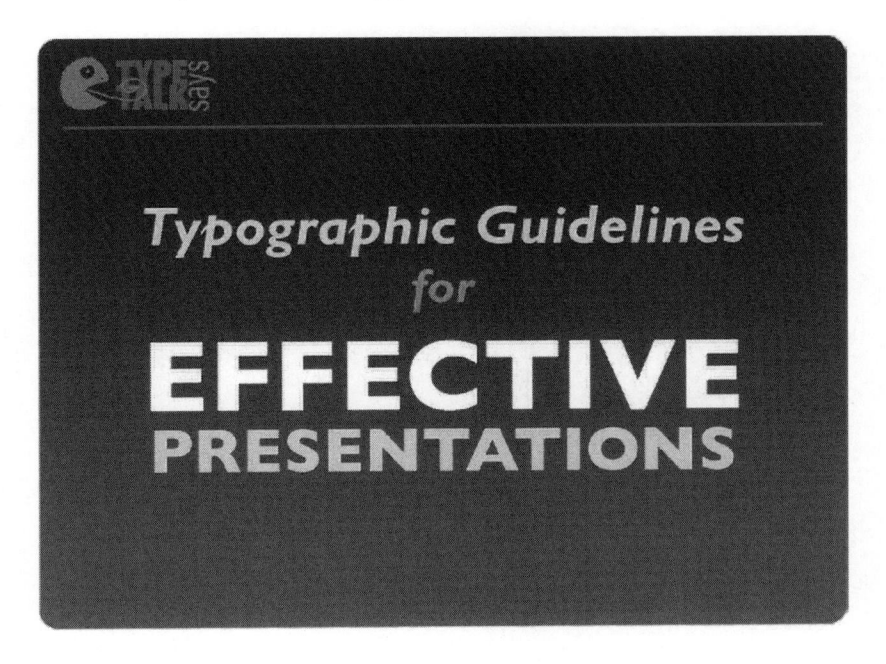

TYPETALK VOLUME 1

Presentation Guidelines
- ✔ 2 typefaces maximum
- ✔ 6 lines of type maximum
- ✔ Keep text large

Presentation Guidelines
- ✔ Keep lines short
- ✔ Maximize contrast
- ✔ Minimize clutter

22

Designing for the Aging Eye

As we age, our eyes and vision change, making it more difficult to read and, for some, to perceive color and contrast. As with any audience, if yours includes seniors, you have to consciously consider certain behaviors and needs in order to attract, engage, and hold your readers' attention. Whether it be for books, magazines, menus, flyers, posters, labels, or signage, the responsible designer will address the needs of their audience, and make senior-friendly type and design choices to help keep reading pleasurable, as well as to enhance understanding and absorption of your message.

Here are some guidelines for setting typography targeted towards the aging eye and those with some degree of visual impairment. Note: If designing for readers with more specific visual impairments or limitations, be sure to do your research, as the situation might call for a different approach to maximize legibility and readability.

Typeface

Use clean, simple, easy-to-read typefaces. Sans serifs are recommended for text for the more visually challenged.

TYPETALK VOLUME 1

Avoid type designs with high contrast and ultra-thin strokes or condensed or expanded designs, especially for text. Stick to those with uniform proportions, open counters, and easily recognizable features. Note that typestyles with taller x-heights have greater readability, especially for text. Avoid fussy scripts, elaborate calligraphic styles, and quirky and hard-to-read designs, even for headlines. Keep the number of fonts per page to a minimum, with two being a good rule of thumb.

> The boy was an orphan, the son of a man who in years gone by had bought and sold lumber throughout the northern section of Maine. His mother had been taken away when he was a small lad, and then he and his father had left town and come to live in the big cabin from which Andy was now trudging so rapidly.
>
> The boy was an orphan, the son of a man who in years gone by had bought and sold lumber throughout the northern section of Maine. His mother had been taken away when he was a small lad, and then he and his father had left town and come to live in the big cabin from which Andy was now trudging so rapidly.

The setting on the left is more challenging to read due to the narrow column width and the typeface's short x-height, tight counters, and decorative characters. The setting on the right, with its clean, open characters and generous type size and line spacing, is much easier to read.

DESIGNING FOR THE AGING EYE

Resist the temptation to use display typefaces with reduced legibility, including those that are highly decorative or ornamental, have interior shading, or are extremely extended or condensed, all of which can be challenging for the senior reader.

Type Size

Bigger is better when it comes to type size for seniors. For some readers, a minimum of 12-point text on 15 points of leading is a good starting point (although exact sizes may vary depending on the typeface that you choose). For the more visually challenged reader with low vision or with degenerative eye conditions, 16- or 18-point type (or even larger) with generous leading might be preferable.

Weight

Don't go too light or too heavy for body text; aim for the middle, such as a book or regular weight. Avoid ultra-thin or extremely heavy weights for both text and display. Use boldface to emphasize a word or a small group of words. Keep the use of italics to a minimum; research indicates that italic type is 18 percent more difficult to read than Roman (upright) letters.

Type formatting

Stick with upper and lowercase when setting continuous text. All-cap settings are harder to read, so save them for only the briefest headlines and signage. Keep the overall letterspacing generous (but not "letterspaced" or tracked out) for maximum character recognition. For the greatest readability, set text left/rag right at a moderate line length, avoiding column widths that are very narrow or extremely wide.

Color and Contrast

The way one sees and perceives color and contrast can become compromised for the visually impaired and those with aging eyes. For this reason, maintain high contrast between type and background, and keep medium-value colors to a minimum. Black (or very dark) type on a white or very light background is the easiest to read. Avoid reverse or dropped-out text, which is more difficult to read. In addition, steer clear of busy background patterns and brightly-colored paper for flyers and such.

> Welcome To Our Newest Residents
> Welcome To Our Newest Residents

Even the most friendly and legible of typefaces can be harder to read when there isn't enough color contrast.

> Welcome To Our Newest Residents
> Welcome To Our Newest Residents

The same type treatment, but with stronger color contrast makes these headlines inviting and easy to read for senior readers.

Break up your text

Avoid long blocks of unbroken text, which can tire the eye and tax the brain. Break copy into chunks wherever possible: use subheads, bulleted lists, boxes, and charts to organize content into smaller units. Information hierarchy should be very clear and easily understood. Make sure to design with lots of white space to reduce eye fatigue.

TYPETALK VOLUME 1

Trick-or-Treat

We invite our residents' families, staff members' children and community neighbors to parade our hallways and show off their costumes while they fill their goody bags. It promises to be a fun-filled, entertaining event. Parents and grandparents are asked to RSVP at (253) 667-0096 and please escort their children during the festivities.

Trick-or-Treat

We invite our residents' families, staff members' children and community neighbors to parade our hallways and show off their costumes while they fill their goody bags. It promises to be a fun-filled, entertaining event.

★ ★ ★ ★ ★

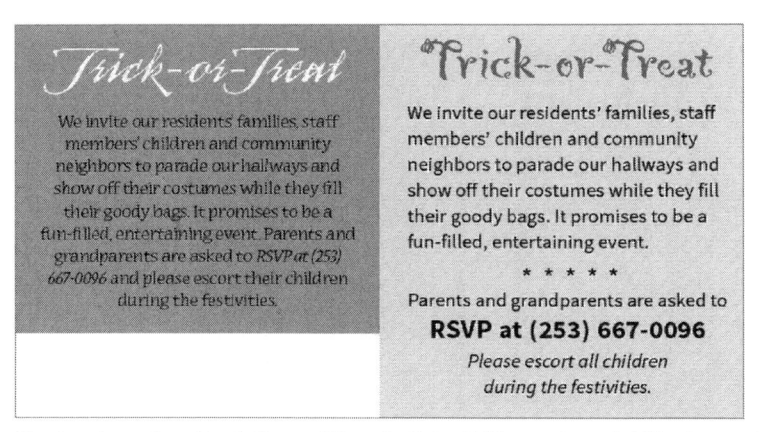

Parents and grandparents are asked to
RSVP at (253) 667-0096
*Please escort all children
during the festivities.*

The treatment on the left sacrifices both legibility and readability in an effort to capture the spirit of the holiday. The setting on the right is much improved (and still conveys Halloween), with its legible typefaces, generous type size and line spacing, flush-left alignment, greater color contrast, chunked-up text, and emphasis on the important information.

Forms

Forms with fields requiring signatures or other information to should be wide and include generous line spacing in order to accommodate a larger handwriting. In addition, make sure the instructions and field labels are clear enough to be easily read.

When setting forms for the senior reader, make the type easy to read and the lines and line spacing generous.

23

Footnotes and Endnotes

Footnotes and their cousin, endnotes, are explanatory notes or references that provide additional information about a point made in the main text. Footnotes appear at the bottom of a page, while endnotes are grouped together at the end of a chapter, section, article, document, or book.

Text to be footnoted is usually indicated with a superscript numeral or other symbol placed immediately after it. The same numeral or symbol also precedes the footnoted reference at the bottom of the page. When there are just one or two footnotes on a page, you can indicate them with a dagger, asterisk, or other symbol. When there are several, it's best to use numerals. Endnotes should always have numerals to allow for easy reference to the main text.

You should set footnotes and endnotes slightly smaller than the body text—usually about two points smaller, as long as they remain readable. The line spacing can be a bit tighter than that of the body text, but this will vary based on the legibility and proportions of the typeface. Set footnotes and endnotes in the same type family as the body text. In some instances, you can use a heavier weight or even an italic for better legibility, readability, and fit.

> ¹Text to be footnoted is usually indicated with a superscript numeral or other symbol placed immediately after it. The same numeral or symbol also precedes the footnoted reference at the bottom of the page.
>
> *When there are just one or two footnotes on a page, they can be indicated with a dagger, asterisk, or other symbol. But when there are several, it is best to use numerals.*
>
> †Endnotes, which are grouped together at the end of a section, should always have numerals to allow for easy reference to the main text.

Footnotes can be indicated with a superscript numeral (top), an asterisk (middle), or a dagger (bottom). Set in TypeCulture's Expo Serif Pro.
Note: I enlarged the size of these examples so you can see them easily on your monitor. I don't recommend this size for footnotes in your projects.

Unless the job or client in question has specific guidelines for footnotes and endnotes, which is often the case with academic and legal documents, use your judgment with respect to maintaining the overall readability of footnotes and endnotes.

24

How to Create Sharp Digital Type Images

Images that contain type make frequent appearances on websites and blogs, ebooks, smartphones, emails, and other digital media. Whether you are a print designer, a business owner with a website, a corporate marketing person, or just someone who has a blog, knowing how to create and supply images for uploading is critical. Even web masters, programmers, and creative directors (who rarely get that involved in a website's production) need to stay current on what kind of images appear sharp and crisp on today's array of devices, specifically retina displays and other high-res technology. I have seen too many websites and other digital media with inappropriate low-res images, which are poor quality, hard to read, and amateurish.

Prior to the availability of high-res monitors, smartphones, e-readers, and the like, the standard "deliverable" for digital images has been a GIF, JPG, or PNG at 72 ppi (pixels per inch) resolution, supplied at the exact required dimensions in pixels. In spite of this, and even before today's higher-res devices, it is easy to find websites and other digital media with fuzzy, hard-to-read logos and other images with type. Some have clearly been enlarged from a smaller image supplied by a client.

I found the image on the left on the web, at this size. It clearly is poor quality, and possibly was enlarged from a much smaller image. In my search for a sharper version, I was able to find the one on the right, which is better, but still not as sharp as it should be. To avoid this, always go back to the designer to get original art when making a new image.

With the development of so many high-res devices and monitors, there is an opportunity for viewers to see crisper, sharper images, which is especially beneficial for those containing type—especially small type.

But you also don't want to repeatedly use images that are too large, because they will cause your web pages to load slowly, frustrating your viewers (or causing them to leave). Web pages that load slower are also penalized by appearing lower in Google search rankings. So you have to try to strike a balance between the quality that your audience expects, and the time it takes to deliver that quality over the internet.

Which format to use?

Each file format has different characteristics and rendering capabilities, but many of their differences are subtle

HOW TO CREATE SHARP DIGITAL TYPE IMAGES

in certain kinds of images. Even so, it is a good idea to know the differences when making images for digital media. Although the focus of this article is on images with type, text can appear with photos, illustrations, or any other kind of graphic, so the format needs to work with everything.

GIF (Graphics Interchange Format): Maximum 256 predetermined colors, good for flat images with solid colors, and when you want to keep the file size small. Largely replaced by PNG.

JPG, or JPEG (Joint Photographic Experts Group): Millions of colors, good for images with photographs and gradients.

PNG-8 (Portable Network Graphics): Maximum 256 colors, similar to GIFs.

PNG-24: Unlimited colors, also reproduces transparency. PNGs are beginning to replace GIFs and JPGs.

SVG (Scalable Vector Graphics): Vector format, not bitmap as all of the above. This advanced format requires more backend work, as it needs to be coded and embedded into the HTML. Stay away from this unless you are working with an experienced web programmer.

    Some clients or environments require a specific format and maximum size. If this is the case, go ahead and create what is asked for. But if it is up to you, play around and use whichever gives you the best results.

Here is a sampling of how different formats and sizes can affect the quality of an image, including the sharpness of the edges and the smoothness of the color blends. All images were created at 72 resolution, or ppi (pixels per inch).

When combining type with an image, the format needs to be right for both. GIF is a poor choice for this 600 px image, as there are not enough colors to create a sharp, crisp image with smooth color blends either for the photo or the type. You can see that the quality suffers, especially in the sky area.

The PNG-8 format is not good for this image either, as there are not enough colors to represent the entire image sharply and smoothly.

HOW TO CREATE SHARP DIGITAL TYPE IMAGES

This 600 px JPG (top) looks much better, as does the PNG-24 (bottom). In fact, they are identical to the average eye.

This PNG-24 file was created 2x up at 1200 px wide, as recommended, and it is much sharper for high-res devices.

Enlarging a 600 px image to 1200 just makes it worse—never scale up a pixelated format.

This is an enlarged comparison of these formats.

How to convert images

If your primary concern is quality and not search engine rankings (or bandwidth cost), I suggest making the image

HOW TO CREATE SHARP DIGITAL TYPE IMAGES

at least two times the final desired size in pixels (if possible based on the size of the original). This will make the image much more sharp on high-res displays, which is particularly important for type. For instance, I received an email for the CA Typography Competition with a graphic that is 1200 pixels wide.

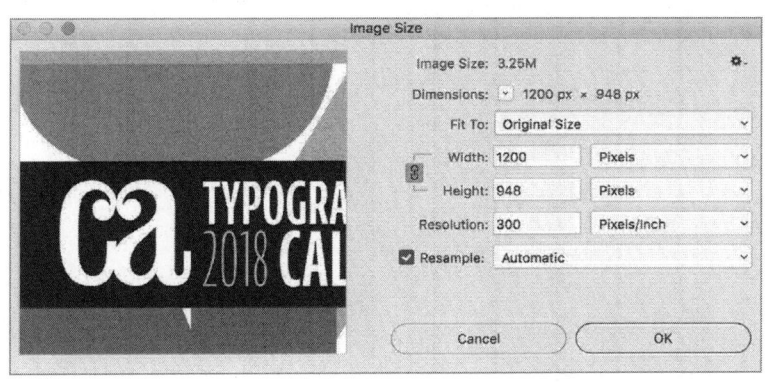

I received an email with the top image. When I opened it in Photoshop (below it), I found it was 1200 px wide. There is nothing wrong with this, as it ensures the image will be sharp on all devices—as long as bandwidth is not a concern.

TYPETALK VOLUME 1

Here's another example.

Helvetica

There were a king with a large jaw and a queen with a plain face, on the throne of England; there were a king with a large jaw and a queen with a fair face, on the throne of France. In both countries it was clearer than crystal to the lords of the State preserves of loaves and fishes, that things in general were settled for ever.

This image was created for this exact size, 600 px. It will not look sharp on high-res devices.

Helvetica

There were a king with a large jaw and a queen with a plain face, on the throne of England; there were a king with a large jaw and a queen with a fair face, on the throne of France. In both countries it was clearer than crystal to the lords of the State preserves of loaves and fishes, that things in general were settled for ever.

This image was created at 1200 px wide. It looks much sharper on many modern displays.

HOW TO CREATE SHARP DIGITAL TYPE IMAGES

Dos and Don'ts

- Try to strike a balance between the quality your audience expects and the costs of larger file sizes in terms of bandwidth and search engine rankings.
- Never make an image smaller than the largest size you might need. In other words, always prepare for the largest possible size and highest resolution.
- Never enlarge an existing web image.
- If an image with small, detailed type will be clickable, go even larger.
- Never use a low-res image for print. (I have seen dozens of print ads using the low-res images from their website and such.)

Keep in mind that many designers, web programmers, and anyone who has a blog or manages their own site might not be aware that they should be making or supplying all images to accommodate high-res devices. For the best final outcome, it makes sense for all people involved in the process be aware of this, and as such, to be informed of the guidelines above.

25

Fun with Pattern Fonts

When we talk about fonts, most people assume we are talking about type characters. But a font can be used to display more than the alphabet. Take, for example, pattern fonts. Pattern fonts consist of decorative or illustrative elements which, when repeated (or tiled) vertically and/or horizontally, create a perfectly seamlessly aligned pattern which can be used for a wide range of purposes to liven up your designs.

One of the most common uses for patterns is to create backgrounds for websites, blogs, and social media pages. While innumerable background images can be found on the web, they are usually JPEG files with fixed sizes and colors, which limit their usage. Pattern fonts offer ease of use as well as unlimited flexibility by allowing you to change their size, proportion, color, and transparency. You also have the option of intermixing them to create your own uniquely personal pattern.

Pattern fonts can also be used for a lot more than just web page backgrounds. They are great for print projects such as menus, signage, invitations, bookplates, posters, packaging, book covers, and editorial pages, as well as fabric and clothing, wallpaper, logos, branding, identity, and so on.

FUN WITH PATTERN FONTS

Pattern fonts are also great for borders and as individual icons or decorative elements. Some even come with corner elements. With a little ingenuity, they can be used as a fill for headline type. They can set the mood of a genre or a time period, from traditional to modern, simple to fancy, geometric to organic to abstract. They can be combined, overlapped, and overlaid... your imagination is the limit.

One very beautiful and useful pattern font series is Wallflowers I, II, and III, designed by Laura Worthington. Although primarily known for her script and handwriting fonts, this talented typeface designer and hand-lettering artist lovingly created these unique, hand-drawn wallpaper tiles and accompanying icons. Floral motifs, abstracts, skeletons, lipstick kisses, even insects—she's got them all! They are super easy to use as they all come with a PDF User Guide that includes a key for accessing every image, as well as samples of the pattern they create.

Many pattern fonts are designed to line up when set with no tracking, and set solid, but not all work this way. Depending on the application you are using, be sure to adjust tracking and line spacing accordingly to make sure the pieces line up correctly. Viewing on your computer monitor at 100% magnification can make the pieces of the pattern look misaligned, even when they are not. To get an accurate view, either zoom in close or print the pattern on a high-resolution printer to see how the pieces actually align.

The Art & Heart of Being Decorative

TRY IT, YOU'LL LIKE IT

YOU CAN BE CURLICUE TOO!

For the background of this image, I used an intricate lace tile from Wallflowers III, as it fit the vintage mood I sought to create. Regarding this design, Laura says, "It took forever to draw, and required lots of research on how lace is made; I even went to a sewing store to look at samples of lace to figure it out!"

Several more patterns from the Wallflower III series by Laura Worthington.

FUN WITH PATTERN FONTS

From intricate pencil sketch to final artwork, this fantasy scene is another Wallflowers image.

Patterns from two ornament fonts by Akira Kobayashi: ITC Seven Treasures (top row) and ITC Japanese Garden (bottom row).

TYPETALK VOLUME 1

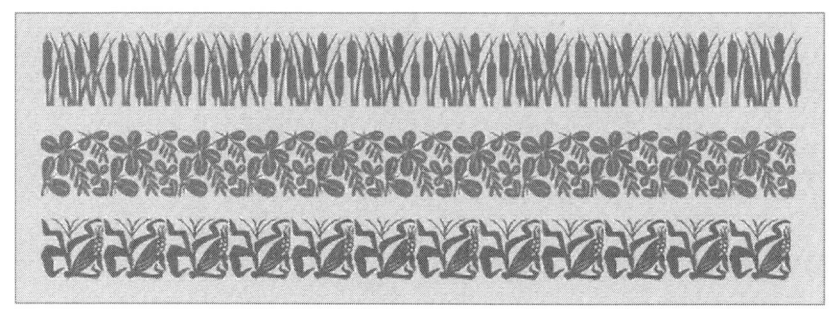

Blooming Meadow, a pattern font designed by Viktor Kharyk, contains many images inspired by nature.

Garamono, a pattern font designed by Khaito Gengo, contains a broad variety of pattern styles.

Printed in Poland
by Amazon Fulfillment
Poland Sp. z o.o., Wrocław